Karl Marx

Profiles in
ECONOMICS

Milton Friedman

John Maynard Keynes

Karl Marx

Adam Smith

Karl Marx

Wolfgang Rössig

MORGAN REYNOLDS PUBLISHING

Greensboro, NC

Dedication:
To Karine-Isabella

Morgan Reynolds Publishing
620 South Elm Street, Suite 387
Greensboro, NC 27406
www.morganreynolds.com
1-800-535-1504

First printing

1 3 5 7 9 8 6 4 2

Library of Congress Cataloging-in-Publication Data

  Rössig, Wolfgang.
    Profiles in economics : Karl Marx / by Wolfgang Rössig. — 1st ed.
       p. cm.
    Includes bibliographical references and index.
    ISBN 978-1-59935-132-2 (alk. paper)
    1. Marx, Karl, 1818-1883—Juvenile literature. 2. Communists—Germany—
  Biography—Juvenile literature. 3. Philosophers—Germany—Biography—
  Juvenile literature. I. Title.
    HX39.5.R59 2009
    335.4092—dc22
    [B]
                                        2009029563

TABLE OF CONTENTS

Early Years

Since Martin Luther, no German thinker has had a greater influence on the world than Karl Marx. His ideas transformed the study of economics, history, sociology, and even literature. But Marx's influence was not confined to students and scholars. His goal, he famously noted, was not to explain the world but to change it. More than a billion people have read his *Communist Manifesto*, which urged oppressed and exploited workers to rise up and overthrow the established order. Revolutionaries all over the globe would heed the call, and by the middle of the twentieth century, governments that professed adherence to his ideas ruled half the world's population.

Karl Heinrich Marx was born in Trier, a German city located on the banks of the Moselle River, on May 5, 1818. He was the third of nine children of Heinrich and Henriette Marx. Five of the Marx children—including Karl's three brothers—would die young, and as an adult Karl was not particularly close to his three surviving sisters, Sophie, Luise, and Emilie.

Though Karl Marx would spend much of his adult life railing against the bourgeoisie—the property-owning middle class—his family was middle class and respectable. His father was a prosperous lawyer who served as counselor-at-law to the High Court of Appeal in Trier, practiced in the Trier County Court, and for many years served as president of the city lawyers' association. In 1819, the year after Karl's birth, Heinrich Marx moved his family from a rented home into a ten-room house he bought at Simeonstrasse 8, near the Porta Nigra, Trier's Roman-era city gate. The new home had a cottage on the grounds, and the Marx household included two maids. The Marx family also owned a vineyard near Trier.

Both of Karl Marx's parents had deep Jewish roots. Heinrich, born Herschel Mordechai Marx in 1777,

Karl Marx was born in 1818 in this house on Brückenstrasse in Trier. The house is now a museum.

Trier had about 15,000 residents when Marx lived there. This view of the city is from 1832.

came from a prominent Jewish family whose members had for generations given Europe important rabbis. Henriette Pressburg Marx, born in Holland in 1788, was the daughter of a rabbi who had himself come from a long line of rabbis.

Herschel Marx and Henriette Pressburg had been married in a Jewish ceremony, but by the time of Karl's birth they were no longer practicing Jews. In fact, Herschel had changed his first name to Heinrich and converted to Christianity. His reasons for conversion were principally economic. In 1815 the Rhineland region where Trier is located had become a part of Prussia, and the Prussian ruler, King Friedrich Wilhelm III, soon signed an edict taking away many of the rights and freedoms of Jews. Among other restrictions, Jews were forbidden to practice law, so to avoid losing his livelihood, Heinrich Marx became a Lutheran, the Protestant denomination favored by the king. Karl and his siblings were baptized into the Lutheran faith in August 1824, shortly before Karl was admitted to primary school. Henriette Marx waited another year before being baptized, presumably out of respect for her father, who was still alive.

The adult Karl Marx never emphasized his Jewish heritage. In fact, his essay "On the Jewish Question," first published in 1844, reveals anti-Semitic tendencies, and his letters contain innumerable derogatory epithets about Jewish rivals. Nor did Marx follow the Lutheran faith in which he was nominally raised. Rather, he was an atheist who believed that people create God in their own image and that religion stands in the way of human freedom.

Relatively little is known about Karl Marx's childhood. Life in the Marx household seems to have been happy and harmonious, though Karl apparently bullied his sisters somewhat—for example, by making them eat cakes made with dirty dough. Of all the Marx children, Karl alone displayed unusual intellectual gifts. This, along with the fact that he was the oldest son (his brother Moritz-David having died at age four in 1818), made Karl the focus of his parents' ambitions.

Heinrich Marx hoped that his son would study law and pursue a legal career, and in addition to paying for Karl's education, he offered frequent advice. For his part, Karl appears to have held his tolerant, well-read, and cultured father in high esteem; he carried a daguerreotype (an early version of a photograph) of Heinrich in his wallet his entire life. By contrast, Karl never developed a strong bond with his mother, whose letters indicate that she was neither well educated nor a deep thinker.

From 1830 to 1835, after he had completed his primary school education, Marx spent five years at the Friedrich Wilhelm Gymnasium in Trier. (A German gymnasium is roughly equivalent to an American college prep school.) Only the best pupils were sent to the gymnasium, because it was expensive.

Marx was a rather good student. He excelled at history and did exceptionally well in Latin and Greek, translating the classics with proficiency and care. He devoured the poetry and plays of such authors as Goethe, Schiller, Dante, Shakespeare, and Aristophanes, and his love of literature is evident in his own writings, which are peppered with quotes from and allusions to the works of these eminent writers. Marx did fairly well in French, geography, and mathematics, but his skills in physics were not so impressive.

The earliest surviving documents in Marx's handwriting are essays he wrote while at Friedrich Wilhelm Gymnasium. One of them, "Considerations of a Young Man on Choosing His Career," reveals his youthful idealism. The seventeen-year-old observed that "we cannot always attain the position to which we believe we are called; our relations in society have to some extent already begun to be established before we are in a position to determine them." Man, Marx went on to say, should not seek to attain a brilliant social position, but

Marx attended the Friedrich Wilhelm Gymnasium (shown here) between 1830 and 1835.

rather strive for fulfillment and to work for the good of humanity:

> According to History the greatest men are those that have worked for the general good and ennobled themselves. Experience calls him the happiest who has made most people happy. Religion itself teaches us that the Ideal towards which all strive sacrificed Himself for humanity, and who shall dare to contradict such claims? If we have chosen the position in which we can accomplish the most for humanity, then we can never be crushed by the burdens because these are only sacrifices made for the sake of all. Then it is no poor, restricted, egoistic joy that we savor; on the contrary our happiness belongs to millions, our deeds live on calmly with endless effect, and our ashes will be moistened by the ardent tears of noble men.

With just one exception, Marx did not strike up any lasting friendships during his youth. Most of his classmates at the Friedrich Wilhelm Gymnasium came from a lower social station—they were the sons of artisans and peasants, and they were able to attend the gymnasium

The first page of an idealistic essay Marx wrote at age seventeen, "Considerations of a Young Man on Choosing His Career." In the essay, written in his native German, the young Marx proposes that people should apply their particular talents for the good of humanity, as this is the surest way to self-fulfillment.

only because of scholarships from the Catholic Church. About half of them would pursue a religious career. (Although Lutheranism was the state religion of Prussia, Catholicism was prevalent in the Rhineland, and the great majority of Trier's approximately 15,000 residents were Catholic.)

Marx's one enduring friendship from his youth was with someone from a different—albeit higher—social station. Edgar von Westphalen was the son of a Prussian baron who served on the king's privy council in Trier. It was Edgar who introduced Marx to the writings of Shakespeare, who would remain his favorite author throughout his life. Marx admired Edgar's father, Ludwig von Westphalen, a kind and cultivated man who spoke German and English equally well, read Latin and Greek fluently, and particularly liked romantic poetry. Later in life, Marx would fondly recall making regular visits to the stately Westphalen home. There he spent many happy hours discussing subjects ranging from literature to history with Edgar and Ludwig von Westphalen—to whom Marx would dedicate his doctoral thesis, referring to the baron as a dear fatherly friend and a living example that idealism was no mere illusion. His friendship with Edgar and admiration for Ludwig von Westphalen aside, Marx had another strong reason for making his pilgrimages to the Westphalen home: Edgar's older sister, Jenny. A close friend of Marx's older sister, Sophie, Jenny was considered one of the most beautiful women in Trier.

In early 1835, as his final months at Friedrich Wilhelm Gymnasium approached, Karl Marx had plans to continue his education. To be eligible for admission at a university, however, Marx would have to pass mandatory final examinations (called an *Abitur*). One-third of the gymnasium students would fail these rigorous academic tests. The studious Karl Marx was not among that group.

2 The Student

On an October morning in 1835, the entire Marx family awoke at four o'clock to say good-bye to seventeen-year-old Karl, who was headed to the university. The Rhineland did not have a train system, and traveling in a stagecoach took many days. The most convenient way to travel was by boat. From Trier, Marx took a steamer boat to Koblenz—a sixteen-hour journey. The next day, he traveled in another boat down the Rhine River to reach Bonn.

Bonn, located some fifteen miles south of Cologne, was scarcely larger than Trier. But its university, with seven hundred students, ranked as the intellectual center of the Rhineland. Three days after leaving his hometown, Marx took up residence in a house already occupied by a fellow student from Trier. He registered himself as a student in the Law Faculty at the University of Bonn.

In his first semester, an enthusiastic Marx put himself down for no less than nine lectures, three of them in the field of philosophy. Baron von Westphalen had aroused in Marx an enthusiasm for romanticism, and Marx attended the popular lectures on philosophy and

Bonn, circa 1840. Marx studied at the city's university for one year.

literature given by the revered August Wilhelm Schlegel. Heinrich Marx advised his son to reduce the workload to six lectures, which Karl did, although he didn't drop any of the non-legal subjects. His first end-of-term report attested that he followed all six courses with zeal and attention.

During the second term, however, Marx reduced the number of lectures to four and gave much less time to formal studies. He had better things to do: enjoying the student life and writing poetry. In these times, students usually had money to spend, and with a generous subsidy provided by his father, Karl was no exception. In Bonn, Marx developed his lifelong habit of spending more money than he could afford.

Marx joined the thirty-member Trier Tavern Club, quickly rising to become one of its five presidents. Like other tavern clubs, its main activity was heavy drinking. One day Marx was arrested and sent to a university jail for disturbing the peace. Conditions in the jail, called a *Karzer* in German, were anything but harsh. In the twenty-four hours of his confinement, Marx was visited by friends who helped him pass the time by playing cards . . . and drinking beer.

Yet membership in a tavern club could have more serious consequences. Rival clubs sometimes clashed, and in 1836 Marx was wounded above the left eye in a saber duel with a member of the aristocratic Prussian Borussia-Korps (whose members, unlike Marx, were expert fencers).

While saber duels were accepted behavior among students, duels with pistols were illegal. When Cologne police caught Marx with pistols, which he was about to

This drawing depicts an 1836 outing of the Trier Tavern Club. Marx became one of the drinking club's presidents.

use in a duel, his father had to convince the examining magistrate to quietly drop the charges.

Heinrich Marx wasn't happy about his son's student life. After one semester, Karl had already gone through the 160 talers that were meant to last a full year. He requested more money without ever bothering to explain how he had spent the 160 talers.

But Marx's father had more to worry about than his son's free-spending ways. Karl spent more time writing poetry

Karl Marx as a university student, 1836.

than studying law. He joined a club of like-minded students and soon wrote a romantic hodgepodge of exalted verses. He wrote about the beauty of nature, rivers in moonlight, enchanted harps, betrayed love, medieval knights, fairies, mermaids, sirens, and the like.

In his rare letters home, he included samples of his poems, which his father scarcely acknowledged. When Marx asked his father to finance the printing of his poetry, a deeply worried Heinrich Marx warned his son: "Although I am very pleased with your poetical gifts and have great hopes of them, I would be very sorry to see you cut in public the figure of a minor poet."

Heinrich Marx also counseled his son to pay attention to his health—though he also found a physician who would attest that Karl was physically unfit for service in the Prussian military. Shortly after his eighteenth birthday, Marx was excused from the army because of a weak chest.

Believing that extracurricular temptations such as beerhouse brawls and poetry clubs were distracting his gifted son from his future career as a lawyer, Heinrich Marx decided that a change was in order. He decided to pull Karl out of the University of Bonn after just a year. Following the 1836 summer holidays, Karl would be sent to the University of Berlin, which had the reputation of being a demanding, no-nonsense institution. In this setting, Heinrich Marx hoped, Karl would be able to concentrate fully on his law studies.

However, the plan ran into an unexpected obstacle: Karl Marx had fallen in love. The object of his affection was Johanna Bertha Julie Jenny von Westphalen. Marx had known Jenny von Westphalen, the older sister of his friend Edgar, from childhood. With her dark auburn hair, green eyes, and fine face, Jenny was strikingly beautiful. She was also intelligent, freethinking, and—as the daughter of Baron Ludwig von Westphalen—a member of an important, aristocratic family. There was every reason to believe she would enter into a socially advantageous marriage, and many men had courted her.

In the end, however, it was Karl Marx who won her heart. He had wooed Jenny before leaving Trier for the University of Bonn, and during the summer of 1836 they became engaged. Marx was eighteen and Jenny twenty-two.

This portrait of Jenny von Westphalen was painted in 1835, the year before she and Karl Marx became engaged.

Marx's parents were initially mortified by the engagement, and not because Jenny was of a higher social class. Marx hadn't asked Baron von Westphalen's permission for his daughter's hand, and for months he and Jenny kept their engagement secret from Jenny's family, which evidently caused Heinrich and Henriette Marx great embarrassment. Jenny's father would finally give his consent to the union in March 1837, although the marriage was still years away.

Marx's summer of love only increased his taste for romanticism and poetry. In a ten-page letter to his father, Marx recounted his feelings during the 650-mile stage-coach journey from Trier to Berlin, which took more than a week. "When I left you, a new world had just begun to exist for me, a world of love that was at first drunk with its own desire and hopeless," Marx wrote.

> Even the journey to Berlin which would otherwise have charmed me completely, excited me to an admiration of nature and inflamed me with a zest for life, left me cold and even, surprisingly, depressed me; for the rocks that I saw were not rougher, not harsher than the emotions of my soul, the broad cities not more full of life than my blood, the tables of the inns not more overladen and indigestible than the stocks of fantasies that I carried with me, nor, finally, was any work of art as beautiful as Jenny.

On October 22, 1836, Marx registered at the University of Berlin. With its 2,100 students, the University of Berlin—founded in 1810—was three times the size of Marx's previous school, the University of Bonn. Berlin, too, was much larger than any city Marx had previously seen. The capital of Prussia, it had more than 300,000 inhabitants, making it the most populous German city.

Although he initially registered as a student in the Law Faculty, over the course of the next four years Marx attended only nine law lectures. Eventually, he also registered in the Faculty of Philosophy. In Marx's mind, legal studies and philosophical speculation were closely intertwined.

A major influence was Professor Eduard Gans, who taught criminal law and Prussian common law. Gans supported a constitutional monarchy. Furthermore, he had celebrated the events of the 1830 July Revolution in France, during which Parisians had risen up and forced the abdication of King Charles X after the king had muzzled the press, dissolved the French legislature, and attempted to limit voting rights. Gans's support for more liberal governance created tensions with the authoritarian Prussian monarchy and earned him a suspension from the university, though he was eventually reinstated. Marx would ultimately come to the view that political reform was desirable but not sufficient to ensure the full emancipation of humanity.

At the University of Berlin, Marx learned to study by excerpting meaningful passages from required readings, something he would do for the rest of his life. While he applied himself to his studies, he also continued to write poems, which he sent to his father and—more important—to Jenny. Though he read Karl's poems, Heinrich advised his son to think about his and Jenny's future.

By the winter of 1837, long hours of studying and writing poetry in the dim light of sooty oil lamps had taken its toll on Marx's health. Fatigued, he was advised to seek recovery in the countryside. He moved to Stralau, a village on a peninsula of the Spree River, a one-hour walk from the Berlin city center. Marx spent all summer in the countryside. His health improved.

Stralau also had a lasting impact on his career. At a local inn, he ran into members of a debating circle of older academics, actors, and writers—the so-called Doctors' Club. They met regularly in a Berlin pub and discussed philosophy and literature. Drama was discussed while the actors recited Shakespeare and Goethe. What all members had in common was an interest in the thought of Georg Wilhelm Friedrich Hegel (1770–1831), the most influential German philosopher of the early nineteenth century.

Stralau was a small, quiet village about an hour's walk from Berlin. After an exhausting year at the University of Berlin, Marx spent the summer of 1837 in Stralau to regain his health.

Marx had read Hegel but had initially dismissed his "grotesque and rocky melody." This disdain wouldn't last. Hegel's philosophy would form the bedrock of Marx's own work.

Hegel's philosophy was grounded in dialectics. As a method of philosophical argumentation, dialectics stretches back to Socrates and other ancient Greek thinkers. In the dialectical method one speaker or writer proposes an idea, or thesis. Another speaker or writer then proposes a counterargument, called the antithesis. This creates a contradiction that eventually results in a synthesis of the two opposing ideas. For Hegel, howeverer, dialectics was not simply a method of philosophical debate. Rather, it was a way to explain change. Change,

Hegel said, occurs when a concept or idea—the thesis— is supplanted by its opposite, or antithesis. While the antithesis may appear to destroy the thesis, in fact both are preserved and integrated within the synthesis. Throughout history, Hegel said, this dialectical process is repeated continuously. In this manner, he believed, history was proceeding in stages, moving inevitably toward the evolution of a cosmic consciousness that Hegel called Absolute Spirit or Mind.

Absolute Spirit was compatible with the idea of God, and in the late 1830s Hegel's followers split into two wings on the subject of religion. The more conservative adherents saw nothing irrational in the traditional representation of religion. By contrast, the more radical followers of Hegel—called the Young Hegelians—sought to destroy what they saw as the outdated dogmas and superstitions of religion. Prominent Young Hegelians included David Friedrich Strauss, Ludwig Feuerbach, and Bruno Bauer, and the Doctors' Club that Marx joined was a focal point of their movement.

In November 1837 Marx wrote to his father and described his explorations of Hegel's writings. He also detailed the progress of his studies in general, mentioned his latest literary efforts, wrote about his plans to become an assistant judge, and even announced his intention to make a surprise visit to Trier in order to cheer up his mother. But once again, he wanted more money—160 talers—having already gone through seven hundred talers while in Berlin. Considering that a Berlin town councilor received eight hundred talers a year, this was no meager sum.

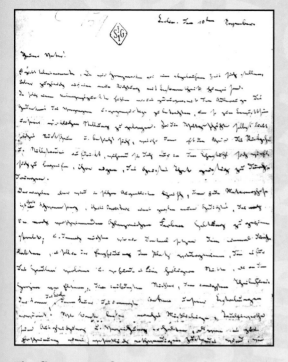

The first page of Marx's November 1837 letter to his father.

In a letter dated December 9, 1837, Heinrich Marx strongly reproached his son for his reckless spending, but he nevertheless sent Karl the 160 talers. He also told Karl to forgo his travel plans and instead visit the family during the next Easter holidays. Heinrich Marx was seriously ill, as he noted in his letter, and he worried about financing Karl's education and seeing him secure a professional position so that he could fulfill the obligations incurred with his engagement to Jenny.

Marx did not come home for Easter, and on May 10, 1838, his father died without having seen his favorite child for nearly two years. Marx didn't even attend his father's funeral—which turned relations with his mother and siblings decidedly sour.

If he hadn't bothered to say good-bye to his father, Marx did said good-bye to his father's ambitions for him. He had already decided to abandon the pursuit of a legal career.

3 Radical Doctor

reed from the expectations of his father, Karl Marx concentrated on philosophy. One professor, Bruno Bauer—who was also a friend of the Doctors' Club—pressed Marx to complete a doctoral dissertation in philosophy. The dissertation was to link the ideas of specific ancient philosophers, such as Socrates and Plato, to the thought of Hegel.

Marx's plan was to get a university post as a lecturer in philosophy. But his timing could not have been more unfortunate, as a thorough purge against the radical Young Hegelians was under way. The Ministry of Education moved Bauer, who had become more and more unpopular in Berlin, to Bonn. Bauer had been in trouble since 1836 for his atheist views, which intensified over the years. Writing that Jesus was a myth—a second-century fusion of Jewish, Greek, and Roman theology—certainly hadn't improved his standing. When another prominent Hegelian at the University of Berlin, Professor Eduard Gans, died unexpectedly in 1839, he was replaced by an archconservative, Friedrich Julius Stahl.

In 1840, a year after the death of Gans, King Friedrich Wilhelm IV acceded to the throne in Prussia.

The new king imposed strict censorship on all publications. Soon, academic freedom was only a distant memory. Marx was disgusted at this turn of events and felt little inclination to attend a university he believed was being run by reactionaries. He focused on his doctoral thesis when not drinking, smoking, and talking with his kindred souls at the Doctors' Club.

Marx thought his future was secure. Once his dissertation was approved, Bruno Bauer would be waiting with the offer of a lecturer's job at the University of Bonn. The problem was that, with the conservative shift at the University of Berlin, there was nobody left on the faculty who would be inclined to accept Marx's dissertation. Stahl would not have accepted it. F. W. von Schelling, a veteran anti-Hegelian philosopher and a favorite of the new king, probably wouldn't have read more than the first few sentences.

Marx decided to submit his dissertation to a smaller school, the University of Jena, which had a reputation for awarding degrees without delay or debate—although not without charging fees. Only nine days after dispatching his dissertation to Jena, on April 15, 1841, Karl Marx received the written approval for his doctorate. From now on, he was able to call himself *Herr Doktor*. On the certificate he received upon graduating from Berlin, it was noted that he had several times been accused of debts, but had been acquitted of participating in a prohibited student association.

Doctor Marx left Berlin, happy but broke. In the following months, he lived rather aimlessly in Trier, Bonn, and Cologne. His feelings for Jenny were as

QUOD

FELIX FAUSTUMQUE ESSE IUBEAT

SUMMUM NUMEN

AUCTORITATE

HUIC LITTERARUM UNIVERSITATI

AB

FERDINANDO I

IMPERATORE ROMANO GERMANICO

ANNO MDLVII CONCESSA

CLEMENTISSIMIS AUSPICIIS

S E R E N I S S I M O R U M

MAGNI DUCIS ET DUCUM SAXONIAE

NUTRITORUM ACADEMIAE IENENSIS

MUNIFICENTISSIMORUM

RECTORE ACADEMIAE MAGNIFICENTISSIMO

AUGUSTO ET POTENTISSIMO PRINCIPE AC DOMINO

CAROLO FRIDERICO

MAGNO DUCE SAXONIAE VIMARIENSIUM ATQUE ISENACENSIUM PRINCIPE LANDGRAVIO THURINGIAE
MARCHIONE MISNIAE PRINCIPALI DIGNITATE COMITE HENNEBERGAE
DYNASTA BLANKENHAYNII KRONTADII AC TAUTENBURGI

PRORECTORE ACADEMIAE MAGNIFICO

VIRO PERILLUSTRI ATQUE AMPLISSIMO

ERNESTO REINHOLDO

PHILOSOPHIAE DOCTORE ARTIUMQUE LIBERALIUM MAGISTRO
MAGNI DUCIS SAXONIAE VIMARIENSIS ET ISENACENSIS A CONSILIIS AULAE INTIMIS PHILOSOPHIAE PROFESSORE PUBLICO ORDINARIO

DECANO ORDINIS PHILOSOPHORUM ET BRABEUTA

MAXIME SPECTABILI

VIRO PERILLUSTRI ATQUE EXCELLENTISSIMO

CAROLO FRIDERICO BACHMANNO

PHILOSOPHIAE DOCTORE

SERENISSIMI DUCIS SAX ALTENBURGENSIS A CONSILIIS AULAE INTIMIS MORALIUM ET POLITICES PROFESSORE PUBLICO ORDINARIO INSTITUTORUM
MAGNIDUCALIUM MINERALOGICORUM DIRECTORE INSTITUTI HISTORICI PARISIENSIS SOCIETATI CAESARKAE PETROPOLITANAE MINERALOGICAE
REGIAE DRESDENSIS MINERALOGICAE POLYTECHNICAE PARISIENSIS ARTIUM ET SCIENTIARUM PUBLICAE APUD TRAIECTINOS ARTIUM ET LITTERARUM
GANDAVIENSIS SCIENTIARUM ET ARTIUM ANTVERPIENSIS MEDICORUM ET PHYSICORUM BRUXELLENSIS DOCTRINARUM DE RERUM NATURA
PHILADELPHIENSIS IN AMERICA SEPTENTRIONALI ET LATINAE IENENSIS ALIARUMQUE SOCIO

ORDO PHILOSOPHORUM

VIRO PRAENOBILISSIMO ATQUE DOCTISSIMO

CAROLO HENRICO MARX

TREVIRENSI

DOCTORIS PHILOSOPHIAE HONORES

DIGNITATEM IURA ET PRIVILEGIA

INGENII DOCTRINAE ET VIRTUTIS SPECTATAE INSIGNIA ET ORNAMENTA

DETULIT

D E L A T A

PUBLICO HOC DIPLOMATE

CUI IMPRESSUM EST SIGNUM ORDINIS PHILOSOPHORUM

PROMULGAVIT

IENAE DIE XV M. APRILIS A. MDCCCXLI.

TYPIS BRANIL

Marx had little chance of getting his doctorate from the University of Berlin after conservatives gained key posts in the philosophy department there. He submitted his dissertation to the University of Jena, and it was quickly accepted. Seen here is Marx's doctorate diploma from Jena, dated April 15, 1841.

strong as ever, and Jenny loved her "Moor," as she affectionately called Marx because of his swarthy complexion and thick black hair. But marriage was out of the question until he found gainful employment. The death of Ludwig von Westphalen in 1842 didn't make things easier. Jenny's family believed that the baron should have seen his daughter's wedding, and Henriette Marx was intensely embarrassed that her son's irresponsibility had prevented that from happening. Reacting to her embarrassment, Marx's mother stopped her son's allowance and withheld his share of Heinrich Marx's estate.

Marx, however, had ambitious plans. He wanted to enlarge his thesis into a professorial dissertation about the history of Greek philosophy, which he planned to present in Bonn.

In February 1842, Marx made his first forays into journalism. For the new Young Hegelian journal, the *Deutsche Jahrbücher* (German yearbooks), Marx wrote a scathing polemic against the latest censorship instructions issued in Prussia. Since the law forbade attacks on the Christian religion and penalized offenses against discipline, morals, and loyalty to the government, there wasn't much left to write about for a critical mind. Even the great moral thinkers of the past—Kant, Fichte, and Spinoza, for example—would have run afoul of these laws, Marx explained. The censor didn't like the essay, and the text wasn't published until 1843, and then only in Switzerland.

Marx also planned to publish a magazine called *Archiv für Atheismus* (Archive for atheism) with Bauer and other provocateurs. However, Bauer's luck was about to run out. He had been able to teach at the University of Bonn because that school had two theological faculties, one Catholic and one Lutheran. Because the two groups frequently clashed, Bauer was safe as long as they couldn't agree on a joint move against him. His downfall was the result of a parody he wrote entitled "The Trumpet of the Last Judgment Against Hegel the Atheist and the Anti-Christ." At first glance, it read like a pious attack written by a devout Christian who wished to prove that Hegel was a revolutionary atheist. In reality, Bauer's purpose was to poke fun at Christianity, and the authorities soon recognized this. The theological faculties seethed with anger and finally united against Bauer. At their request, the Prussian king expelled Bauer from the University of Bonn in May 1842.

Marx had lost his sponsor. Now an academic career was suddenly out of reach. But he didn't worry. Gainful employment had come to him in Cologne, the wealthiest and largest city in the Rhineland, where people were openly talking about democracy, a free press, and a unified Germany. In 1841, a group of wealthy manufacturers had founded the liberal newspaper *Rheinische Zeitung* (Rhenish newspaper). Marx was hired as an editor of the newspaper, which was staffed by some of his friends from the Doctors' Club. Journalism was going to be his new calling.

4 The Journalist

The *Rheinische Zeitung* was intended to bolster the principle of equality of all citizens before the law. One of the newspaper's founders was the lawyer Georg Jung. He came from a rich Dutch family and was married to the daughter of a banker from Cologne. Because of Jung, money was no issue.

Marx first met Jung in 1841, and the two men struck up a friendship. Marx, already known as a fearsome debater, took part in discussions on the organization of the paper. When Jung had to hire his first editor, he asked Marx for advice. Marx recommended Artur Rutenberg, a Young Hegelian friend from his days in Stralau and the brother-in-law of Bruno Bauer.

Soon after, Marx himself was in desperate need of a job. During the summer of 1842, while he was visiting Trier, quarrels with his mother grew so intense that Marx stormed out of the family house on Simeonstrasse. He stayed at a nearby guesthouse while awaiting the wedding of his sister Sophie.

Marx's friend Bruno Bauer advised him to seek a position on the *Rheinische Zeitung*. Marx took the advice and was hired. Within months, he had total control of the paper. Rutenberg, an alcoholic, had been unable to fulfill his commitments, and Marx was appointed editor-in-chief with an annual salary of five hundred talers. This was the first—and last—time Marx received a salary.

Prussian authorities were alarmed to learn that Marx had taken over the newspaper. He was already under police surveillance for his radical views. Still, the authorities had broad power to suppress opinions they didn't like. Since 1819 the Carlsbad Decrees had been in effect. These regulations stipulated that no newspaper could go to press in any of the major German states without the prior knowledge and approval of state officials. Fighting against the censors became one of Marx's

Cologne was the largest and wealthiest city in the Rhineland. In 1841 Marx went there to work as an editor for the liberal newspaper *Rheinische Zeitung*.

preoccupations. It was no easy task, as censors were known to object to even the most inoffensive of material. For example, one censor prohibited the publication of an advertisement for a German translation of Dante's *The Divine Comedy* because he felt that the divine should not mix with comedy.

Marx's very first journalistic work for the *Rheinische Zeitung* revealed what he had in store for the censor. In a series of five articles, he waged a full frontal attack on the Rhineland Parliament, which upheld the privileged position of the aristocracy. He kicked it off with "Debates on the Freedom of the Press and on the Publication of the Parliamentary Proceedings." The outsmarted censor let the article pass because Marx did not

A woman cuts wood. In the Rhineland, harsh penalties—including prison sentences—were handed out to people caught collecting wood from privately owned forests. Marx railed against the injustice of the situation.

attack the Prussian government directly, but only commented on what the parliamentarians had said.

Of equal importance was the fourth article of the series. It dealt with the introduction of more stringent laws proposed by the Parliament concerning thefts of wood from private forests. The gathering of fallen branches for fuel had traditionally been an unrestricted privilege, but now anyone who picked up a twig could be condemned to prison or compelled to pay the forest owner the value of the wood taken—as assessed by a forester in the employ of the owner. Marx asked: "If every violation of property, without distinction or more precise determination, is theft, would not all private property be theft? Through my private property, do not I deprive another person of this property? Do I not thus violate his right to property?"

At the time, more than four of every five offenses dealt with by the Rhineland courts involved the theft of timber. The legal travesty of people being prosecuted simply for collecting dead wood to heat their homes led Marx to think, for the first time, about questions of class, private property, and the state. He came to see private property as a tool of oppression.

The censor was not amused and banned the other articles of the series. But Marx was not an easy target. Within weeks, the readership of the *Rheinische Zeitung* tripled. Marx insisted on a critical and liberal focus backed by the reporting of facts, not vague reasoning. This put him in disagreement with his former Berlin colleagues, who had formed themselves into a club known as the *Freien* (the Free), the successor to the old Doctors'

Club. They made it a point to criticize everything about the current political system.

By the end of November 1842, the disagreement between Marx and his former colleagues in Berlin led to a permanent estrangement. The total break came after Bruno Bauer had spoken out for the dissolution of the state, private property, and even the family. The Freien wanted Marx to publish articles espousing these views in the *Rheinische Zeitung*. Marx refused, not only because the Freien offered no concrete proposals for what would replace the institutions they wanted abolished but also because Marx recognized that publishing their articles would guarantee that the authorities would shut down the *Rheinische Zeitung*. His former friends condemned him, complaining that he ran his paper like a dictator.

Although he avoided giving a platform to the incendiary views of Bauer and the Freien, Marx nevertheless had constant battles with the censors. He developed ways to get around them. For example, he would send articles to the censor in small sections, hoping that the censor would not understand the articles' full meaning. In this manner, Marx managed to publish pieces that were highly critical of the Prussian monarchy and its authoritarian policies. He also published articles that criticized the tsar, or king, of Russia.

By early 1843, the days of the *Rheinische Zeitung* were numbered. In January, under pressure from the Prussian king, the Saxon government suppressed another liberal periodical, the *Deutsche Jahrbücher*. Only days later, the Prussian Council of Ministers—

This cartoon, published after Prussian authorities shut down the *Rheinische Zeitung*, depicts Marx as a modern Prometheus.

presided over by the king—decided to suppress the *Rheinische Zeitung*. The decision was hastened by angry protests from the Russian government. The date picked for the final issue of the *Rheinische Zeitung* was March 31, 1843.

The end of his newspaper editorship brought greater changes in Marx's life. Arnold Ruge, a philosopher and political writer who had been associated with the defunct *Deutsche Jahrbücher*, had decided to go into exile in Paris. There he planned to publish a new periodical, the *Deutsch-Französische Jahrbücher* (German-French yearbooks). Ruge invited Marx to join him as co-editor. He promised Marx an annual salary of 550 talers, plus royalties.

With the prospect of this fixed income, Marx finally was able to marry Jenny von Westphalen. Throughout their seven-year-long engagement, Jenny had remained

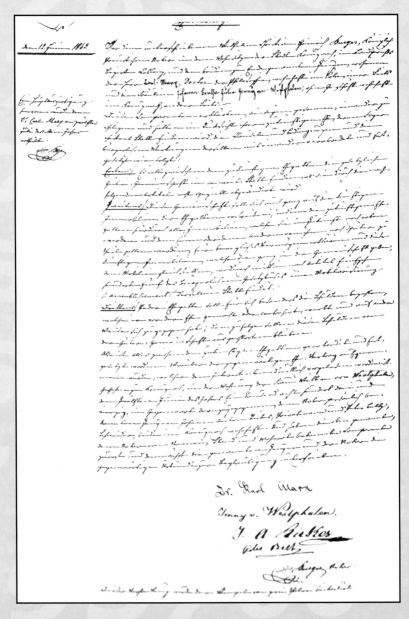

Baroness von Westphalen made her daughter and Marx sign this marriage contract. It made Marx responsible for paying any debts he had incurred before he and Jenny were married.

fiercely loyal to her fiancé. She defended him against all attacks from her aristocratic (and anti-Semitic) relatives, who insisted that a union with Marx was beneath her station.

In June of 1843, to avoid local gossip as well as Jenny's overbearing and archconservative half brother Ferdinand—a career civil servant and future Prussian minister of the interior who was now the head of the von Westphalen family—Jenny and her mother fled to the fashionable spa town of Kreuznach, fifty miles east of Trier. There, on June 19, 1843, Karl Marx and Jenny von Westphalen were married. The bride wore a green silk dress and a garland of pink roses. None of the groom's relatives attended the ceremony. Marx was twenty-five, his wife twenty-nine.

Jenny's mother had insisted that her son-in-law sign a marriage contract promising that, while the couple would have legal common ownership of property, each spouse would pay for his or her own past debts. This attempt to ensure her daughter's financial security did little good. Marx would remain chronically in debt, and he and Jenny would frequently live in poverty.

In terms of financial matters, the honeymoon trip up the Rhine from Kreuznach to Schaffhausen provided a glimpse of what was to come. One wedding present from Jenny's mother was a collection of silver jewelry, a silver plate, and a large box of cash that was meant to help the marriage over the first few months. The newly-weds spent the money in only one week, and the other gifts would wind up in a variety of pawnshops in Frankfurt, Brussels, and London.

5 Revolution Approaches

r. and Mrs. Karl Marx spent the first months of their married life as guests at Jenny's mother's rented house in Kreuznach. Marx was waiting for Ruge's project to materialize. In the evenings, the newlyweds took long walks to the river, listening to the nightingales singing from the woods on the far bank. By day, Marx went about his usual business: reading and writing like a madman. One of his favorite essays was Ludwig Feuerbach's "Preliminary Theses for the Reform of Philosophy," which had been published in Switzerland in February 1843.

In the essay, Feuerbach, who had already criticized the fundamental dogmas of Christianity and questioned the existence of God and the immortality of man, attempted to destroy the abstract concept of "good." Feuerbach held that philosophy should not start from God, or the infinite, but with the finite, the particular, the real. It should also acknowledge the primacy of the senses. Feuerbach was a philosophical materialist who rejected any discussion of abstract principles. In his view, all that can and should be discussed is what exists. "The true relationship of thought to being is this:

being is the subject, thought the predicate," Feuerbach wrote. "Thought arises from being—being does not arise from thought."

Soon, it was time for Karl and Jenny Marx to leave their homeland. In late October, they took a stagecoach to Paris. Thereafter, they would return to Germany only for short visits.

For Marx, Paris was the new capital of a new world. Revolutions in 1789 and 1830 had made it the intellectual center for progressive thinkers from all over Europe. Christian and utopian socialists gathered there, as did communists and anarchists. More than 85,000

A view of Paris in the 1840s. Karl and Jenny Marx moved to the French capital in late 1843.

Germans lived in Paris. Most were artisans, but there were also intellectuals and writers.

Karl and Jenny Marx first lived on Rue Vaneau 23 in the Faubourg St. Germain on the Left Bank of the Seine River, where many artists, writers, and immigrants lived. Initially, they shared a house with two other German couples, including Arnold Ruge and his wife, but the arrangement didn't work out. After only two weeks, the Marxes moved to a house next door. They could afford to splurge since they were living off the one thousand talers Marx had received as severance pay from the *Rheinische Zeitung*.

The following months were the happiest the couple ever enjoyed, and Marx was eager to please his wife, who was pregnant with their first child. A daughter, Jenny Caroline, was born on May 1, 1844. Because the baby was somewhat sickly, Jenny Marx went home to Trier to spend several months with her mother and a wet nurse. The baby's health soon improved.

The German-born poet Heinrich Heine. Marx published work by Heine in the *Deutsch-Französische Jahrbücher*, and the two became friends.

Ruge had not been able to find any French author willing to write for the *Jahrbücher*, which he thought would be necessary to make the publication a success. After he fell ill, Ruge left it up to Marx to edit and publish the first volume.

In the end, the only non-German voice was that of an exiled Russian anarchist, Mikhail Bakunin. The German-born poet Heinrich Heine, who had lived in exile in Paris for decades, played the part of the only "French" author participating in the project.

Marx and Heine would strike up a lasting friendship, which is somewhat surprising given Marx's well-deserved reputation as a pitiless critic and Heine's sensitivity to criticism (he was known to weep when people found fault with his work). For once, however, Marx restrained himself, probably because he had revered Heine's work since childhood. The two also shared a hatred of the stagnant and oppressive political and social conditions in Germany. Heine wrote a long satirical poem, "Germany: A Winter's Tale," which was based on his visit to Germany in 1843. Marx admired the poem.

Another writer published in the *Jahrbücher* was Friedrich Engels. His essay "Outlines of a Critique of Political Economy" deeply impressed Marx and marked the real beginning of Marx's lifelong interest in economic questions.

Engels believed that recurrent economic crises were the result of anarchy in production. The growth and accumulation of capital—money or goods that can be used to produce other goods—involved a lowering of salaries for workers, which intensified a class struggle. Science and technology, which could offer great advancements in the lives of everyone, had instead become a means of oppressing workers even further. Engels was convinced that these conditions would eventually lead to the demise of capitalism, an economic system in which factories and businesses are privately owned, and in which free markets are allowed to operate.

Marx had first met Engels, briefly, in Cologne in 1842. At that time, Marx had distrusted Engels. But two years later, when Engels visited him in Paris during a journey from Germany to England, Marx formed a different opinion. Engels showed Marx his recently published book, *The Condition of the Working Class in England in 1844*, and Marx was impressed. The two men realized that they held identical views on a broad array of philosophical and economic issues, and they began a lifelong friendship. Their collaboration would shake the world.

Engels's father was a wealthy industrialist who operated cotton mills in Germany and Manchester, England. On numerous occasions, money from Engels would save Marx from tumbling into abject poverty. In the copious correspondence between Marx and Engels (about 4,500 letters have survived), Marx often shared the most intimate and embarrassing details about his health and personal misery with his friend.

The goal of the *Deutsch-Französische Jahrbücher* was to introduce the French to German thinking, and to expose Germans to the revolutionary spirit that had existed in France since 1789. But it wasn't to be. The first issue—which turned out to be the last—was a financial disaster. It didn't sell well in France because no French writer was participating, and it was immediately banned in Prussia and the other German states.

Both Marx and Engels believed that mass production led to the alienation and exploitation of workers. Seen here is an English textile factory, circa 1845.

The Prussian government even proclaimed that its contents were an incitement to high treason and ordered Marx, Ruge, and Heine to be arrested if they attempted to return to their fatherland. In Austria, severe penalties were threatened against any bookseller caught stocking the newspaper.

Co-publisher Julius Froebel gave up first, saying that he didn't want to lose more money. A frightened Ruge was next. He suspended the publication and refused to pay Marx the promised salary because Marx's articles were far too revolutionary. Furthermore, he charged that Marx had failed to finish anything because he'd strayed from his work and "plunged again and again into an endless sea of books." The folding of the *Deutsch-Französische Jahrbücher* left Marx with no money. As "severance pay" he was given unsold copies of the journal, which were essentially worthless.

There was some truth to Ruge's claims about Marx's voracious reading habits during his brief editorship of the *Jahrbücher*. Marx focused especially on books about national economy and socialism. His English was still rather poor, but he devoured the works of British economists, such as Adam Smith and David Ricardo, in French translations. Marx had by now begun to turn away from liberalism, an ideology that opposed authoritarian governments and championed liberty, or the freedom of individuals to live their lives as they saw fit. At the time, the right to own property was viewed as essential to individual freedom. While Marx continued to oppose authoritarian governments, he rejected the connection between property rights and freedom and began advocating the total elimination of private property—the foundation of communism. For Marx, communism—an economic system in which goods are owned by all members of society and are available to all as needed—was the only solution to the conflicts that plagued humanity.

In 1844, Marx started developing his ideas about capitalism and communism in a series of handwritten manuscripts that went unpublished during the author's lifetime. Parts have been lost, but the existing manuscripts were collected and published during the twentieth century under the title *Economic and Philosophic Manuscripts of 1844*. When he wrote the manuscripts,

Marx was still just twenty-six years old, but scholars see in these early writings the groundwork for his mature thought, and especially the foundations of his 1867 masterwork, *Capital*. One important theme Marx elucidated in his 1844 manuscripts was the alienation of workers under capitalism.

Before the advent of capitalism, Marx noted, goods were made in homes and small workshops owned by artisans, who had freedom to set their own hours and conditions of work. Artisans also had the ability to shape the products of their work, because they were involved in the process from start to finish. A cooper, for example, split and planed logs; measured, cut, and notched the staves; made the barrelheads; fitted the pieces together; and finally secured the barrel with metal hoops. A shoemaker fashioned the uppers and the soles, stitched them together, and added any adornment. Under this system of production, craftspeople often knew their customers personally, and they had some ability to negotiate the conditions of their compensation (for example, through money or bartering).

All that changed, Marx observed, with the coming of capitalism, which gave rise to large factories where goods were mass-produced rather than crafted individually by artisans. The factory worker was reduced to a small—and replaceable—component in a vast and impersonal production process, performing the same discrete task over and over again each shift. The factory owner set the work hours (which were typically long), working conditions (which were typically difficult), and wages (which were typically low). Under these circumstances, Marx said, workers inevitably became alienated, or estranged, from their work, from other people, even from human nature itself.

Marx's time in Paris did not last far beyond 1844, when he wrote *The Economic and Philosophic Manuscripts*. He had contributed a satirical piece attacking King Friedrich Wilhelm IV of Prussia to a biweekly magazine called *Vorwärts* (Ahead), published by German emigrant Heinrich Börnstein. Marx may have thought France's freedom of the press would protect him from retaliation, but he was wrong. On January 7, 1845, Prussian envoy Alexander von Humboldt presented King Louis Philippe in Paris with two items—a valuable vase from the Royal Prussian Porcelain Manufacture, and a handwritten letter from Friedrich Wilhelm IV protesting the outrageous insults and libels published by *Vorwärts*. In response, Louis Philippe ordered the shutdown of the magazine—which Prussian spies erroneously

Helene Demuth, sent from Trier by Jenny's mother, became the Marx family's faithful housekeeper. She remained with the family for almost forty years.

reported was run by Marx—and told his interior minister, François Guizot, to expel Marx from France.

Marx had only twenty-four hours to leave. As he quickly found out, the only country on the continent that would accept radical political refugees was Belgium. Still, Marx had to sign a written promise that on his word of honor, he would not publish in Belgium any political work. Jenny stayed behind in Paris for a few days to sell off the household goods. When she arrived in Brussels, her husband was already busy with reading, writing, card playing, and drinking. Jenny was pregnant with her second child, and her mother sent her a maidservant from Trier, Helene Demuth.

Helene, age twenty-five at the time, would spend the rest of her life in the Marx household, which she ran with admirable efficiency and dignity even in moments of greatest misery. Sometimes when the Marxes had no money at all, "Lenchen," as Helene was nicknamed, managed to put food on the table. For now, however, the Marx family did have money. Marx had received from a publisher in Darmstadt a 1,500-taler advance for a planned (though never completed) book about political and national economy. Engels had given him an additional thousand talers.

The Marxes hoped to settle in Brussels, but Engels foresaw trouble. "I fear that in the end you'll be molested in Belgium too," he wrote to Marx in a letter completed March 7, 1845, "so that you'll be left with no alternative but England."

6 The Revolutionary

Prussian police continued to harass Marx in Belgium. Spies kept a close watch on him and reported all his activities, however mundane. On several occasions, the Prussian government asked Belgian authorities to expel Marx, who was wanted in Prussia for charges of "high treason." To end the persecution, Marx even thought (or at least pretended to think) about immigrating to the United States.

Despite the near-constant harassment, the Marxes were able to live rather comfortably in Belgium for a while. Between Karl's advance from the publisher in Darmstadt and proceeds from Jenny's sale of the household furniture and linens in Paris, they had enough money to rent a house. Finding a place to live took some time, however, because Jenny had very precise ideas about what she wanted in a new home. While her husband searched for a suitable house, the family lodged in hotels or the spare rooms of friends. Finally, after about six months, Marx found a modest house at 5 Rûe d'Alliance at the eastern end of Brussels.

Meanwhile, Jenny had gone to Trier to visit with her mother. She returned to Brussels just in time to deliver her second daughter, Laura, in September 1845. Two years later a son, Edgar, was born.

As his family was growing, Marx was busy with his writing. In 1845 he and Engels—who had also moved to Brussels—collaborated on *The German Ideology*, a book that would not be published until the 1930s. *The German Ideology* criticized—often in a bitingly satirical manner—German philosophers such as the Young Hegelians Ludwig Feuerbach and Bruno Bauer and the anarchist Max Stirner. It also sketched out Marx's "materialist conception of history," by which he explained and analyzed the progress of human societies in economic terms—specifically, according to how people collectively

In 1845 the Marx family moved into this house at 5 Rue d'Alliance in Brussels.

produce the goods they need given the methods of production available at a particular stage of development. According to the materialist conception of history (or what would later be called historical materialism), consciousness does not exist independent of the material world but instead arises from it. Social relations are driven first and foremost by the material conditions of humans—not by ideas, religious beliefs, political ideologies, or other forces.

Increasingly, Marx was concerned with changing society, and in *The German Ideology* he presented a vision of how communism would eliminate the alienation of workers by doing away with the strict division of labor characteristic of capitalism:

> In communist society, where nobody has one exclusive sphere of activity but each can become accomplished in any branch he wishes, society regulates the general production and thus makes it possible for me to do one thing today and another tomorrow, to hunt in the morning, fish in the afternoon, rear cattle in the evening, criticize after dinner, just as I have a mind, without ever becoming hunter, fisherman, cowboy or critic.

Marx imagined an egalitarian society (a society in which all people are equal). When a friend suggested that she could not imagine Marx living contentedly in such a society, Marx nodded. "These times will come, but we must be away by then," he said. In other words, he wouldn't want to live in the type of society he was advocating for others.

In summer 1845, Marx and Engels traveled to London and Manchester for six weeks. They spent most of their time in Manchester's Chetham's Library, where

View of a park and government buildings in Brussels, capital of Belgium, where Marx and Engels lived from 1845 to 1848.

they studied the works of several eminent national economists.

On their way back to Belgium, they met with leading representatives of the British Chartists in London. Chartism was a movement for political and social reform in the United Kingdom and was one of the first mass working-class labor movements in the world. Chartists demanded universal suffrage (voting rights for all), limitation of work hours, higher salaries, and labor protection laws.

Another meeting in London was with the German Workers' Educational Association. This organization was an offspring of the clandestine League of the Just, which had plotted conspiracies in Paris before several of its leaders fled to England in 1839. From London, they had created a network of supporters in Switzerland, Germany, and France. Where law banned

Edgar von Westphalen, Marx's boyhood friend and brother-in-law, was a founding member of the Brussels Committee of the League of the Just.

workers' associations, their "lodges" masqueraded as choral societies or gymnastic clubs. The League of the Just's most important thinker was Wilhelm Weitling, a tailor who had published his book *Mankind as It Is and as It Ought to Be* in 1838.

Marx and Engels suggested supporting the work of the League of the Just by setting up correspondence committees all over western Europe. The committees would maintain a continuous interchange of letters with the League of the Just and other similar associations in western Europe.

In December 1845, with the Prussian police continuing to demand his extradition, Marx gave up his Prussian citizenship. For the rest of his life, he would be a man without a country. He twice tried, in 1848 and 1861, to get back his Prussian citizenship, but those efforts proved unsuccessful. He also filed for British naturalization in 1874, but his application was denied because he had "behaved disloyally towards his King."

Early in 1846, Marx and Engels invited Wilhelm Weitling to become a founding member of the Brussels Committee of the League of the Just, and Weitling agreed. All other Communist parties would ultimately descend from this group. In addition to Marx, Engels, and Weitling, the eighteen founding signatories of the

Brussels Committee included Jenny Marx, Edgar von Westphalen, and Ferdinand Freiligrath.

The Brussels Committee's meeting of March 30, 1846, started a tradition that future Communist cells and parties would hold dear: purging anyone suspected of deviation from official correctness. In this case the target was Weitling, whom Marx despised for the superficiality of his ideas and for his preachy attitude. Far from supporting Weitling's League of the Just, Marx and Engels had been planning a hostile takeover. An outside observer, a young Russian named Pavel Annenkov, gave a fascinating report of the meeting in which the coup was pulled off, as well as a vivid characterization of Marx in these times:

> Marx himself was the type of man who is made up of energy, will, and unshakable conviction. He was most remarkable in his appearance. He had a shock of deep black hair and hairy hands and his coat was buttoned wrong; but he looked like a man with the right and power to demand respect, no matter how he appeared before you and no matter what he did. His movements were clumsy but confident and self-reliant, his ways defied the usual conventions in human relations, but they were dignified and somewhat disdainful; his sharp metallic voice was wonderfully adapted to the radical judgments that he passed on persons and things. He always spoke in imperative words that would brook no contradiction and were made all the sharper by the almost painful impression of the tone, which ran through everything he said. This tone expressed the firm conviction of his mission to dominate men's minds and prescribe them their laws. Before me stood the embodiment of a democratic dictator such as one might imagine in a day dream.

In the meeting, a sarcastic Marx accused Weitling of rousing the workers without offering any scientific ideas

Wilhelm Weitling, author of *Mankind as It Is and as It Ought to Be*, was the League of the Just's leading thinker. Marx believed Weitling's ideas to be superficial and detested his preachy attitude.

or constructive doctrine to guide them, which could only lead to their ruin. This, he said, was "equivalent to vain dishonest play at preaching which assumes an inspired prophet on the one side and on the other only the gaping asses." Politically, Weitling was finished; soon after, he was expelled from the Brussels Committee.

As he still cherished the idea of bringing German and French radicals together, Marx invited Pierre-Joseph Proudhon, the leading French socialist theoretician of his time, to join the Brussels Committee of the League of the Just and to organize a committee in Paris. Proudhon declined, earning him Marx's disdain.

Marx attacked Proudhon's newly published *The Philosophy of Poverty* with a hundred-page pamphlet called *The Poverty of Philosophy*, published in Paris and Brussels in June 1847. In the pamphlet Marx also personally attacked Proudhon—who had warned against revolutionary violence—for meekly accepting the status quo. More important, however, *The Poverty of Philosophy* contained the first public statement of Marx's materialist conception of history (as *The German Ideology* remained unpublished). "M. Proudhon the economist understands very well that men make cloth, linen, or silk materials in definite relations of production," Marx wrote.

> However, what he has not understood is that these definite social relations are just as much produced by men as linen, flax, etc. Social relations are closely bound up with productive forces. In acquiring new productive forces, men change their mode of production; and in changing their mode of production, in changing the way of earning their living, they change all their social relations. The hand-mill gives you society with the feudal lord; the steam-mill, society with the industrial capitalist.

The Poverty of Philosophy is also the first public statement of the central idea of the more famous *Communist Manifesto*: that the antagonism between the proletariat (workers) and the bourgeoisie (property owners) was a struggle of class against class.

Proudhon never publicly replied to *The Poverty of Philosophy*, but his own copy is filled with angry scribbles in the margins. For years, Marxists and Proudhonists would contend with one another for influence in the international labor movement.

In the meantime, Engels took up the task of organizing a committee of the League of the Just in Paris. At a meeting there in mid-October 1846, he forced the workers present to decide whether they were avowedly Communist and ready to demonstrate their allegiance

Friedrich Engels was Marx's lifelong friend, collaborator, and financial supporter. This photo of Engels is from the mid-1840s.

to their class, or whether they were vaguely "in favor of the good of mankind."

The Paris Committee soon attracted the attention of the French police chief. To avoid being expelled from France, Engels kept a low profile. He stayed away from the league for a while and spent his free time carousing with Parisian women. He raved about the delicious encounters he had enjoyed with Parisian *grisettes*, young working-class women.

While Engels was enjoying women and wine in Paris, Marx could not even afford to go to London, where the League of the Just had organized a June conference to discuss a merger with the Brussels group. The meeting turned out to be a takeover by the Brussels Committee, and a new name was adopted. The League of the Just was renamed the Communist League. The old league slogan, "All Men Are Brothers," was also replaced. Marx had already said that he knew many men he did not want as brothers. The new slogan became "Working Men of All Countries, Unite!"

Marx was elected president of the Brussels branch (or "community") of the secretive league. He also founded a more open and less political Workers' Association.

Engels created a draft statement of principles for the new Communist League, which circulated among all communities in Europe for consideration. In November 1847, Engels paid for Marx to travel to London to take part in the ten-day congress of the German Workers' Educational Association, which had its headquarters above the Red Lion pub on Great Windmill Street in Soho. In a memoir written years later, Friedrich Lessner, a journeyman tailor from Hamburg who was living in London in 1847, described Marx's dominant presence:

> Marx was then still a young man, about 28 years old, but he greatly impressed us all. He was of medium height, broad-shouldered, powerful in build, and vigorous in his movements. His forehead was high and finely shaped, his hair thick and pitch-black, his gaze piercing. His mouth already had the sarcastic curl that his opponents feared so much. Marx was a born leader of the people. His speech was brief, convincing and compelling in its logic. He never said a superfluous word; every sentence contained an idea and every idea was an essential link in the chain of his argument. Marx had nothing of the dreamer about him.

Marx gave an impressive speech in London. As a result, he was asked to write a pamphlet that was meant to introduce to the public the unanimously approved principles of the semi-clandestine Communist League.

7 The Communist Manifesto

Marx did not rush to write the Communist League's new manifesto, or declaration of principles. The London Central Committee of the Communist League began to grow impatient. On January 24, 1848, the London Central Committee sent an ultimatum to the regional committee in Brussels. "If the Manifesto of the Communist Party, the writing of which he [Marx] undertook to do at the recent congress, does not reach London by 1 February of the current year," the ultimatum said, "further measures will have to be taken against him. In the event of Citizen Marx not fulfilling his task, the Central Committee requests the immediate return of the documents placed at Citizen Marx's disposal."

The warning worked. Within one week, in his study at 42 Rue d'Orléans, Marx managed to write perhaps the most important political pamphlet in world history, consuming countless bad cigars in the process. While Engels appears on the title page as coauthor, Marx did the actual writing.

The Manifesto of the Communist Party—which is most often referred to simply as *The Communist Manifesto*—

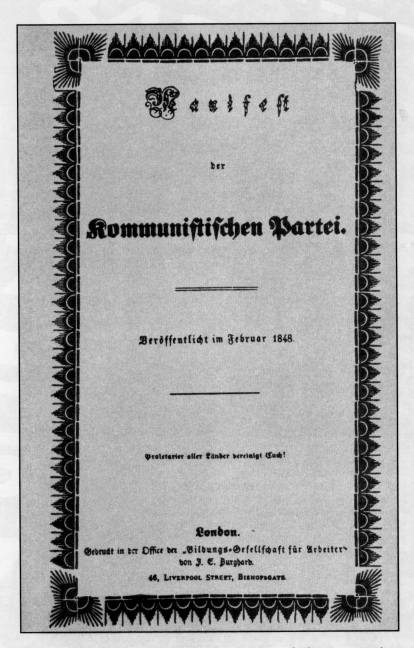

The cover of the German-language version of *The Communist Manifesto*, arguably the most influential political pamphlet in history. Marx wrote the classic statement of Communist principles in just one week.

begins with a rhetorical flourish that has been quoted countless times: "A spectre is haunting Europe—the spectre of Communism."

Four sections follow the short introduction. The first begins with the now-famous assertion, "The history of all hitherto existing society is the history of class struggles."

Marx then briefly describes the varied socioeconomic structures of previous eras. "In the earlier epochs of history," he says, "we find almost everywhere a complicated arrangement of society into various orders, a manifold gradation of social rank." Ancient Rome, for instance, had patricians, knights, plebeians, and slaves. Society during the Middle Ages was composed of feudal lords, their landowning noble vassals, and serfs bound to the land, as well as guild-masters, journeymen, and apprentices who worked in trades in the cities.

From the perspective of class, the distinctive feature of the modern era, according to Marx, was that society was increasingly being divided into just two classes: the bourgeoisie, who owned property, including the factories that produced goods; and the proletariat, or working class, who toiled in factories for low wages. In 1848, when Marx wrote *The Communist Manifesto*, the proletariat made up only a small part of the population of Europe. Many people were members of a middle class consisting of small-business owners, shopkeepers, artisans, tradesmen, and so on. However, Marx believed that these people too would eventually sink into the ranks of the proletariat. The specialized skills of artisans, for example, were of little value in an era of mass production, in which factory machines, operated by low-wage, unskilled workers could produce goods at a much lower cost. After the lower strata of the middle class had been forced into the proletariat, Marx predicted, small-scale factory owners and capitalists would be put out of business by big capitalists—and they, too, would become part of the proletariat. With many workers competing for jobs, the capitalists could keep wages low—just enough for workers to survive and, through their labor, to earn more profits for the capitalists. Wealth would be concentrated in the hands of an ever-smaller group, while the masses of people would live in abject misery.

Ultimately, however, Marx prophesied that members of the proletariat would be driven together by their awful plight. Inevitably, he said, the proletariat would rise up and overthrow the bourgeoisie.

A copy of the only existing manuscript page of *The Communist Manifesto* in Marx's handwriting. The two lines at the top were written by his wife, Jenny.

Marx predicted that members of the working classes would eventually rise up against the bourgeoisie and seize their factories and property. In the Communist system proposed by Marx, the state would control all property and means of production, and would allocate resources according to the needs of the proletariat.

In the second section of *The Communist Manifesto,* Marx describes the relationship of the Communists to the proletarians. Essentially, he says, the Communists represent the most advanced of the working-class parties, though Communists "have no interests separate and apart from those of the proletariat as a whole."

Marx says that "the theory of the Communists may be summed up in the single sentence: Abolition of private property." He then goes on to refute bourgeois objections to communism.

Marx describes how the proletariat will wrest power from the bourgeoisie. He further outlines the measures that would be taken by the proletariat once it had ⌐ ⌐ ⌐ ⌐ ⌐ ⌐ ⌐ ⌐ ⌐ ⌐ ourgeoisie. These measures include the ⌐ ⌐ ⌐ ⌐ ⌐ ⌐ ⌐ ⌐ ⌐ pital from the bourgeoisie to the proletari- ⌐ ⌐ ⌐ ⌐ ⌐ ⌐ ⌐ ⌐ ation of all instruments of production in ⌐ ⌐ ⌐ ⌐ ⌐ ⌐ ate controlled by the proletariat, and the ⌐ ⌐ ⌐ ⌐ a larger industrial base. Landed wealth

Plato's thoughts on private property

and inheritance would be abolished. The state would own all factories. It is interesting to note that many of the other measures that Marx called for—such as the creation of national banks, the nationalization of the railways, a progressive income tax, and free education—have actually been introduced in all European states.

The third section of *The Communist Manifesto* contained an extended criticism of types of socialism other that the "pure" communism Marx advocated. These included conservative (or bourgeois) socialism and utopian socialism.

The fourth and final section is short. It describes how the Communists should deal with other parties espousing similar ideas. *The Communist Manifesto* ends with the famous sentences:

> The Communists disdain to conceal their views and aims. They openly declare that their ends can be attained only by the forcible overthrow of all existing social conditions. Let the ruling classes tremble at a Communistic revolution. The proletarians have nothing to lose but their chains. They have a world to win.
>
> WORKING MEN OF ALL COUNTRIES, UNITE!

The importance of *The Communist Manifesto* was not that it articulated new ideas. Most of the ideas were already in circulation. What set this pamphlet apart and secured its success were its clarity and the way it powerfully synthesized Communist ideas.

Within weeks of *The Communist Manifesto*'s appearance, significant upheaval in Europe began. On February 25, 1848, revolution wiped away the regime of France's King Louis Philippe and his interior minister,

Guizot, who had ordered troops to open fire on unarmed demonstrators. A few days later, the government in Austria fell, and in Berlin the Prussian king was forced to appoint a liberal government.

Marx was ecstatic. For ten years, he had expected the day of the revolution, and it looked as though that day had finally arrived. More good luck seemed to follow. In mid-February, his mother had sent him the first part of his inheritance—six thousand talers. Marx used part of the money to buy pistols and daggers for the German workers he hoped would rise up in revolt. When they heard this news, the Belgian political police were alarmed. Marx already was under close surveillance for having published incendiary articles, and, of course, the Prussian envoy had been busy denouncing his activities.

March 3, 1848, was an important day in Marx's life. In the morning, he was presented with a letter from Ferdinand Flocon, a member of the provisional government in Paris, which annulled his expulsion from France and invited him to return to Paris. "The soil of the French Republic is a place of refuge for all friends of freedom," Flocon wrote. "Tyranny has banished you, free France opens her doors to you and all those who fight for the holy cause, the fraternal cause of all peoples."

With such a letter in hand, Marx wasn't bothered much when in the afternoon of the same day Belgian immigration police handed over a decree, signed by King Leopold I, that ordered Marx's expulsion from Belgium within twenty-four hours. In the next few hours, it was decided to move the headquarters of the Central

In 1848 Europe was convulsed by a series of revolutions. In this illustration, revolutionaries battle government soldiers at a barricade on a street in Frankfurt.

Committee of the Communist League to Paris. After midnight, ten Belgian police officers stormed Marx's home and arrested him. Marx was dragged off to a prison cell at the town hall, allegedly because his passport was not in order. Several documents were also confiscated and later handed over to the Prussian government.

Jenny was told politely that if she wanted to see her husband, she would have to follow the police officers. But at the police station, she was arrested for not having an identity document with her. Under the ludicrous charge of vagrancy, she was remanded to custody, spending the night in a large holding cell.

The next day, an examining magistrate asked with sarcasm why all those farsighted police officers had not arrested the Marxes' three little children as well. In the

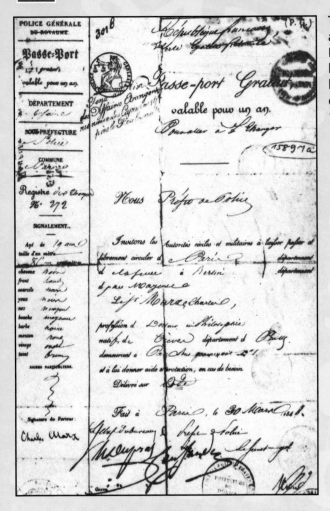

The Belgian authorities issued Marx this passport before expelling him from the country in March 1848.

afternoon, Karl and Jenny Marx were freed and given two hours to leave the country. Jenny hastily disposed of their household items, leaving most of the better linen and the silver with a family friend and selling the rest. Police escorted the family all the way to the French border.

Once in France, the Marx family had to take a horse-drawn carriage because during the unrest that came to be known as the revolutions of 1848, coachmen had uprooted the rail tracks and destroyed the engines of the trains. When the exhausted Marx family finally arrived in Paris, they found the streets still littered with burnt barricades, uprooted paving stones, and shattered glass. The French tricolor—a flag that symbolized the republican ideals of the French Revolution—was flying proudly everywhere.

Marx soon founded the German Workers' Club in Paris. Then, on March 19, 1848, news arrived that revolution had also broken out in Vienna and Berlin. Immediately, a "German Legion" was formed in France. Its members were eager to march into and liberate their homeland. Recruits soon numbered several thousand, and throughout the remainder of the month the German Legion drilled.

France's provisional government was only too happy to see the foreign agitators depart. It granted the German Legion a sum of fifty centimes per man for each day the group spent marching to the frontier. There, tragedy awaited the men. Most members of this quixotic legion did not survive the first encounter with well-trained German soldiers only miles after they had crossed the Rhine River.

Marx and most members of the Communist League had warned against such foolishness. They decided to filter into Germany in small, unarmed groups with the aim of fomenting revolt in their hometowns. Their arms would not be rusting bayonets but agitation and propaganda. Accompanied by his family, Engels, and Ernst Dronke, a young radical writer, Marx first traveled to the city of Mainz. He carried with him *The Communist Manifesto* and a handbill headed "Demands of the Communist Party in Germany." This seventeen-point program, a watered-down version of the manifesto, was meant to win over the bourgeoisie since Germany had a small working class.

Marx's family decided to wait out the events in Trier while Marx went to Cologne and applied for a permit to stay. But four months later, Marx's request to be reinstated as a Prussian citizen was denied. Prussia could expel him anytime if he became too much of a nuisance.

It didn't take Marx long to do just that. With the remaining money from his inheritance, along with funds scraped together from donors, he founded a new daily newspaper, the *Neue Rheinische Zeitung* (New Rhenish newspaper). He served as editor-in-chief, and he ran his radical paper dictatorially.

In late summer 1848, the political situation in Germany grew worse. The inept Prussian government was toppled, but instead of a new liberal government being installed, martial law was declared in Cologne. The military commander immediately suspended publication of the *Neue Rheinische Zeitung*. A warrant was issued for the arrest of Engels, who fled to Belgium. After rude treatment by the Belgian authorities, he continued on to France, where he went on a wine-tasting spree with pretty women before moving on, penniless, to Switzerland.

The *Neue Rheinische Zeitung* resumed publication after the lifting of martial law on October 12, 1848, but the newspaper was inundated with libel suits. Marx spent days in court. He defended himself brilliantly, proving correct his father's belief that he would have made a capable lawyer.

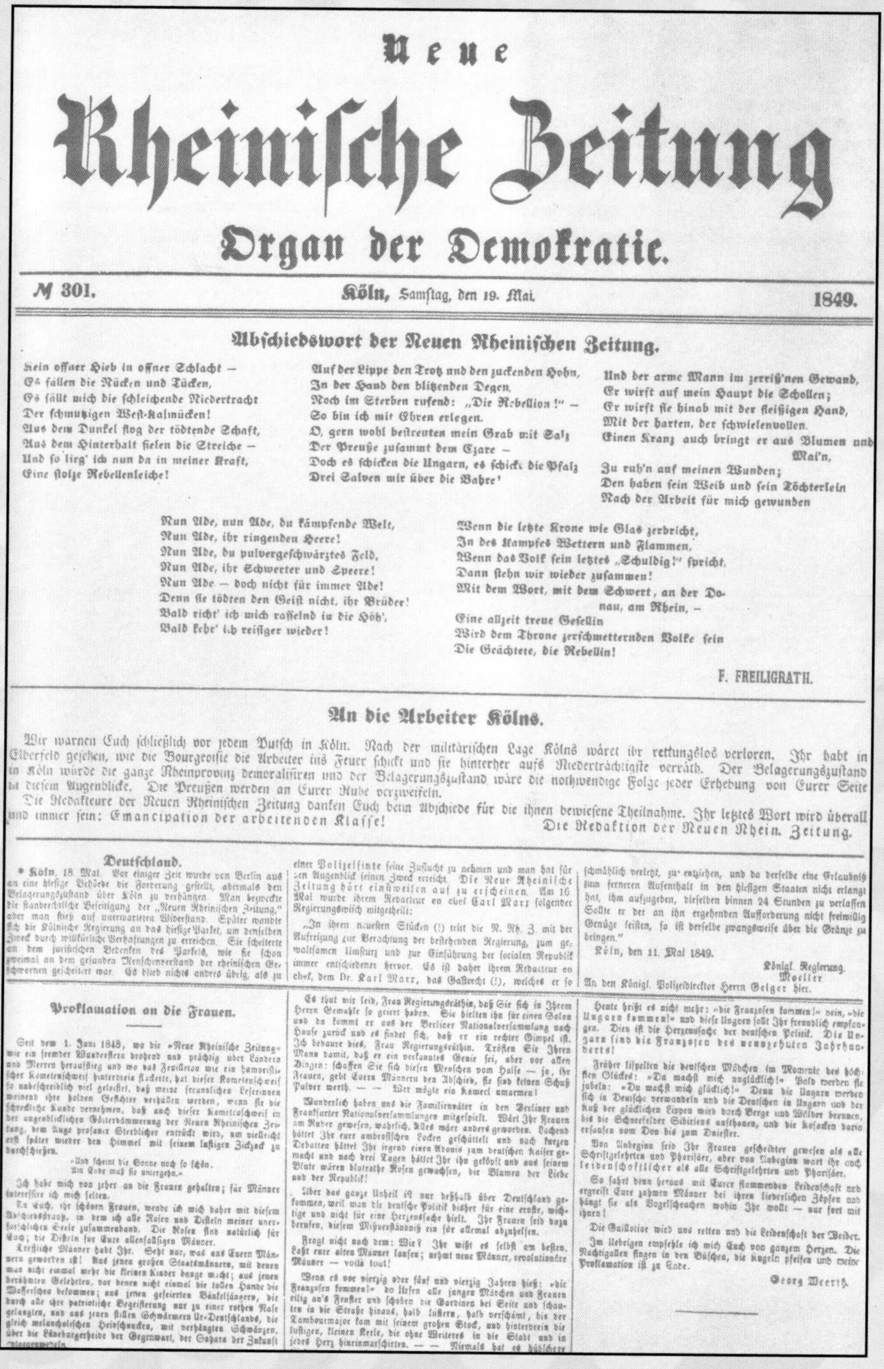

Neue

Rheinische Zeitung

Organ der Demokratie.

№ 301. Köln, Samstag, den 19. Mai. 1849.

Abschiedswort der Neuen Rheinischen Zeitung.

Kein offner Hieb in offner Schlacht –
Es fällen die Nücken und Tücken,
Es fällt mich die schleichende Niedertracht
Der schmutzigen West-Kalmücken!
Aus dem Dunkel flog der tödtende Schaft,
Aus dem Hinterhalt fielen die Streiche –
Und so lieg' ich nun da in meiner Kraft,
Eine stolze Rebellenleiche!

Auf der Lippe den Trotz und den zuckenden Hohn,
In der Hand den blitzenden Degen,
Noch im Sterben rufend: „Die Rebellion!" –
So bin ich mit Ehren erlegen.
O, gern wohl bestreuten mein Grab mit Salz
Der Preuße zusammt dem Czare –
Doch es schicken die Ungarn, es schickt die Pfalz
Drei Salven mir über die Bahre!

Und der arme Mann im zerriß'nen Gewand,
Er wirft auf mein Haupt die Schollen;
Er wirft sie hinab mit der fleißigen Hand,
Mit der harten, der schwielenvollen.
Einen Kranz auch bringt er aus Blumen und Mai'n,
Zu ruh'n auf meinen Wunden;
Den haben sein Weib und sein Töchterlein
Nach der Arbeit für mich gewunden

Nun Ade, nun Ade, du kämpfende Welt,
Nun Ade, ihr ringenden Heere!
Nun Ade, du pulvergeschwärztes Feld,
Nun Ade, ihr Schwerter und Speere!
Nun Ade. – doch nicht für immer Ade!
Denn sie tödten den Geist nicht, ihr Brüder!
Bald richt' ich mich rasselnd in die Höh',
Bald kehr' ich reisiger wieder!

Wenn die letzte Krone wie Glas zerbricht,
In des Kampfes Wettern und Flammen,
Wenn das Volk sein letztes „Schuldig!" spricht,
Dann stehn wir wieder zusammen!
Mit dem Wort, mit dem Schwert, an der Donau, am Rhein, –
Eine allzeit treue Gesellin
Wird dem Throne zerschmetternden Volke sein
Die Geächtete, die Rebellin!

F. FREILIGRATH.

An die Arbeiter Kölns.

Wir warnen Euch schließlich vor jedem Putsch in Köln. Nach der militärischen Lage Kölns wäret ihr rettungslos verloren. Ihr habt in Elberfeld gesehen, wie die Bourgeoisie die Arbeiter ins Feuer schickt und sie hinterher aufs Niederträchtigste verräth. Der Belagerungszustand in Köln würde die ganze Rheinprovinz demoralisiren und der Belagerungszustand wäre die nothwendige Folge jeder Erhebung von Eurer Seite in diesem Augenblicke. Die Preußen werden an Eurer Ruhe verzweifeln.

Die Redakteure der Neuen Rheinischen Zeitung danken Euch beim Abschiede für die ihnen bewiesene Theilnahme. Ihr letztes Wort wird überall und immer sein: Emancipation der arbeitenden Klasse!

Die Redaktion der Neuen Rhein. Zeitung.

Deutschland.

* Köln, 18. Mai. Vor einiger Zeit wurde von Berlin aus an eine hiesige Behörde die Forderung gestellt, abermals den Belagerungszustand über Köln zu verhängen. Man bezweckte die standrechtliche Beseitigung der „Neuen Rheinischen Zeitung," aber man stieß auf unerwarteten Widerstand. Später wandte sich die Kölnische Regierung an das hiesige Parket, um denselben Zweck durch willkürliche Verhaftungen zu erreichen. Sie scheiterte an dem juristischen Bedenken des Parkets, wie sie schon zweimal an dem gesunden Menschenverstand der rheinischen Geschwornen gescheitert war. Es blieb nichts andres übrig, als zu einer Polizeifinte seine Zuflucht zu nehmen und man hat für den Augenblick seinen Zweck erreicht. Die Neue Rheinische Zeitung hört einstweilen auf zu erscheinen. Am 16 Mai wurde ihrem Redacteur en chef Carl Marx folgender Regierungswisch mitgetheilt:

„In ihren neuesten Stücken (!) tritt die N. Rh. Z. mit der Aufreizung zur Verachtung der bestehenden Regierung, zum gewaltsamen Umsturz und zur Einführung der socialen Republik immer entschiedener hervor. Es ist daher ihrem Redacteur en chef, dem Dr. Karl Marx, das Gastrecht (!), welches er so schmählich verletzt, zu entziehen, und da derselbe eine Erlaubniß zum ferneren Aufenthalt in den hiesigen Staaten nicht erlangt hat, ihm aufzugeben, dieselben binnen 24 Stunden zu verlassen. Sollte er der an ihn ergehenden Aufforderung nicht freiwillig Genüge leisten, so ist derselbe zwangsweise über die Gränze zu bringen."

Köln, den 11. Mai 1849.

Königl. Regierung.
Moeller

An den Königl. Polizeidirektor Herrn Geiger hier.

Proklamation an die Frauen.

Seit dem 1. Juni 1848, wo die »Neue Rheinische Zeitung« wie ein fremder Wunderstern drohend und prächtig über Ländern und Meeren heraufstieg und wo das Feuilleton wie ein humoristischer Kometenschweif hinterdrein flackerte, hat dieser Kometenschweif so unbeschreiblich viel geleistet, daß meine freundlichen Leserinnen weinend ihre holden Gesichter verhüllen werden, wenn sie die schreckliche Kunde vernehmen, daß auch dieser Kometenschweif in der augenblicklichen Götterdämmerung der Neuen Rheinischen Zeitung, dem Auge profaner Sterblicher entrückt wird, um vielleicht erst später wieder den Himmel mit seinem lustigen Zickzack zu durchschießen.

»Und scheint die Sonne noch so schön,
Am Ende muß sie untergehn.«

Ich habe mich von jeher an die Frauen gehalten; für Männer interessire ich mich selten.

An euch, ihr schönen Frauen, wende ich mich daher mit diesem Abschiedsstrauß, in dem ich alle Rosen und Disteln meiner unverwüstlichen Seele zusammenband. Die Rosen sind natürlich für Euch; die Disteln für Eure allenfallsigen Männer.

Treffliche Männer habt Ihr. Seht nur, was aus Euern Männern geworden ist! Aus jenen großen Staatsmännern, mit denen man nicht einmal mehr die kleinen Kinder bange macht; aus jenen berühmten Gelehrten, vor denen nicht einmal die tollen Hunde die Wasserscheu bekommen; aus jenen gefeierten Bänkelsängern, die durch alle ihre patriotische Begeisterung nur zu einer rothen Nase gelangten, und aus jenen stillen Schwärmern Ur-Deutschlands, die gleich melancholischen Heidschnucken, mit verhängten Schwänzen, über die Lüneburgerheide der Gegenwart, der Sahara der Zukunft entgegenwedeln.

Es thut mir leid, Frau Regierungsräthin, daß Sie sich in Ihrem Herrn Gemahle so geirrt haben. Sie hielten ihn für einen Solon und da kommt er aus der Berliner Nationalversammlung nach Hause zurück und es findet sich, daß er ein rechter Gimpel ist. Ich bedaure dies, Frau Regierungsräthin. Trösten Sie Ihren Mann damit, daß er ein verkanntes Genie sei, aber vor allen Dingen: schaffen Sie sich diesen Menschen vom Halse — ja, ihr Frauen, gebt Euern Männern den Abschied, sie sind keinen Schuß Pulver werth. — — Wer möchte ein Kameel umarmen!

Wunderlich haben uns die Familienväter in den Berliner und Frankfurter Nationalversammlungen mitgespielt. Wärt Ihr Frauen am Ruder gewesen, wahrlich, Alles wäre anders geworden. Lachend hättet Ihr eure ambrosischen Locken geschüttelt und nach kurzen Debatten hättet Ihr irgend einen Adonis zum deutschen Kaiser gemacht und nach drei Tagen hättet Ihr ihn geköpft und aus seinem Blute wären blutrothe Rosen gewachsen, die Blumen der Liebe und der Republik!

Aber das ganze Unheil ist nur deßhalb über Deutschland gekommen, weil man die deutsche Politik bisher für eine ernste, wichtige und nicht für eine Herzenssache hielt. Ihr Frauen seid dazu berufen, diesem Mißverständniß ein für allemal abzuhelfen.

Fragt nicht nach dem: Wie? Ihr wißt es selbst am besten. Laßt eure alten Männer laufen; nehmt neue Männer, revolutionäre Männer — voilà tout!

Wenn es vor vierzig oder fünf und vierzig Jahren hieß: »die Franzosen kommen!« da liefen alle jungen Mädchen und Frauen eilig an's Fenster und schoben die Gardinen bei Seite und schauten in die Straße hinaus, halb lüstern, halb verschämt, bis der Tambourmajor kam mit seinem großen Stock, und hinterdrein die lustigen, kleinen Kerle, die ohne Weiteres in die Stadt und in jedes Herz hineinmarschirten. — — Niemals hat es hübschere

Heute heißt es nicht mehr: »die Franzosen kommen!« nein, »die Ungarn kommen!« und diese Ungarn sollt Ihr freundlich empfangen. Dies ist die Herzenssache der deutschen Politik. Die Ungarn sind die Franzosen des neunzehnten Jahrhunderts!

Früher lispelten die deutschen Mädchen im Momente des höchsten Glückes: »Du machst mich unglücklich!« Bald werden sie jubeln: »Du machst mich glücklich!« Denn die Ungarn werden sich in Deutsche verwandeln und die Deutschen in Ungarn und der Kuß der glücklichen Lippen wird durch Berge und Wälder brennen, bis die Schneefelder Sibiriens aufthauen, und die Kosacken darin ersaufen vom Don bis zum Dniester.

Von Anbeginn seid Ihr Frauen gescheidter gewesen als alle Schriftgelehrten und Pharisäer, aber von Anbeginn wart ihr auch leidenschaftlicher als alle Schriftgelehrten und Pharisäer.

So fahrt denn heraus mit Eurer flammenden Leidenschaft und ergreift Eure zahmen Männer bei ihren liederlichen Zöpfen und hängt sie als Vogelscheuchen wohin Ihr wollt — nur fort mit ihnen!

Die Guillotine wird uns retten und die Leidenschaft der Weiber.

Im Uebrigen empfehle ich mich Euch von ganzem Herzen. Die Nachtigallen singen in den Büschen, die Kugeln pfeifen und meine Proklamation ist zu Ende.

Georg Weerth.

The final issue of the *Neue Rheinische Zeitung* (May 19, 1849) was printed in red as a protest against censorship by the Prussian government.

In May 1849, revolution broke out again after King Frederick Augustus II of Saxony rejected a proposed liberal constitution and called in Prussian troops to suppress street fighting in the city of Dresden. The unrest soon spread to Prussia, where the authorities quickly moved to shut down the *Neue Rheinische Zeitung*. The Prussian members of the newspaper staff were arrested, while the non-Prussians—including Marx—were ordered deported within twenty-four hours.

After settling his debts, Marx was penniless. Jenny's family silver was sold to a Frankfurt pawnshop, and she and her children took refuge in her mother's home in Trier once again.

Engels returned long enough to fight in four skirmishes against Prussian troops. Then he escaped to Switzerland.

Marx did not see the point in dying for the revolutionary cause and, in June 1849, he traveled to Paris. In July he was joined by Jenny, who was pregnant with the couple's fourth child. Unfortunately, a new French government had taken power and, determined to quell the turmoil, ordered that all suspected revolutionaries—French or foreign—be rounded up. Marx was given a letter banishing him from Paris. He was to go to the malaria-infested swamps of Brittany. He considered this a veiled attempt on his life.

There was now only one country in which Marx could take refuge. On August 27, 1849, he sailed to England.

8 The Economist

Marx didn't expect to stay in England for long. However, fate decided differently. Except for short visits abroad, he would remain in England (mostly in London) for the rest of his life.

The German refugee committee helped him get through his first months in London, and Marx was not worrying much. He, like many other German political refugees, believed that the revolution had merely suffered a temporary setback.

In the meantime, Marx put his energies into a new monthly paper, the *Neue Rheinische Zeitung Politisch-Ökonomische Revue*. The publishers soon ran out of money, however, and the publication did not survive the year 1850.

In his writings from this period, Marx frequently focused on revolutions, which he characterized as the locomotives of history. Revolutions, he believed, moved history from one stage to the next. According to Marx, the true significance of revolutions was less in the political changes they brought than in the economic changes—the changes in modes of production, which in turn produced fundamental social change.

A view of London from around the time Marx arrived there as a political refugee, in 1849. Marx did not expect to stay in England for a long time, but he ended up spending the rest of his life there.

Marx's articles in the *Zeitung Politisch-Ökonomische Revue* gave a sharp analysis of the reasons why the revolutions of 1848 had failed. One article examined the class struggles in France between 1848 and 1850. In 1852, Marx expanded the articles he had written in London to publish a polemic about the victory of the reactionary forces in France. In *The Eighteenth Brumaire of Louis Napoleon*, Marx traced the rise of Louis-Napoleon, the nephew of Napoleon Bonaparte. Unlike his uncle, Louis-Napoleon was a man of mediocre talents. Still, he managed to become president of France before making himself Emperor Napoleon III and—like Napoleon Bonaparte before him—killing parliamentary democracy in the process. Marx was inspired by the idea that all major events in world history happen twice—first as tragedy and then as comedy.

The Eighteenth Brumaire of Louis Napoleon was first printed in a German-language newspaper in New York called *Die Revolution*, which was published by Marx's friend Joseph Weydemeyer. Weydemeyer intended to release *The Eighteenth Brumaire* in book form, but he went broke and was unable to pay the printer, who retained the copies. Only a few copies of the first edition ever made it to Europe. The book was later printed as *The Eighteenth Brumaire of Louis Bonaparte*.

Back in England, Marx believed that he and Engels were under constant surveillance by Prussian spies—a situation the two loudly complained about in a letter to

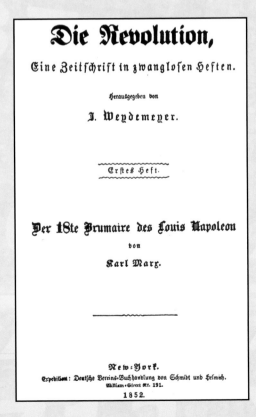

The German-language paper *Die Revolution* ran Marx's *Eighteenth Brumaire of Louis Napoleon* in 1852. Efforts to publish the polemic in book form ran into trouble.

the London magazine *The Spectator*. Though Marx tried to be cautious, several informants succeeded in winning his confidence. The most notorious was Dr. Wilhelm Stieber, who would become the chief of the Prussian police. Stieber was obsessed with uncovering Communist conspiracies. In spring 1851 he received orders from the Prussian minister of the interior to spy on Marx, and if possible to establish a connection between Marx and a failed attempt on the Prussian king's life. At the time, the Marx family was living in a cramped house on Dean Street, in London's squalid Soho district. Stieber managed to infiltrate a meeting of the Communist League that was held there. He reported that the murder of princes was, in fact, discussed and approved at the meeting.

The Prussian authorities wanted Marx extradited. But Home Secretary Sir George Grey, the British official who would have to order the deportation of Marx, refused to do so.

Of course, this did not stop the Prussian authorities from going after Communists whenever they could. In May 1851, police in Saxony arrested a tailor named Peter Nothung, who traveled through the German states on behalf of the Cologne headquarters of the Communist League. The authorities discovered a few copies of *The Communist Manifesto* and a list of German members of the Communist League, including ten from Cologne. This led to numerous house searches and arrests.

Marx organized a committee to raise money for the accused. He also organized a campaign in England to protest the arrests. Jenny wrote about these efforts in a letter to a friend:

> My husband had to work the whole day right through into the night. The whole thing is now a battle between the police on one side and my husband on the other. He is credited with everything, the whole revolution, even the conduct of the trial. A whole office has been established in our house. Two or three do the writing, others run errands, others scrape together pennies so that the writers can continue to exist and bring against the old official world proof of the unheard-of scandal. In the middle of it all my three faithful children sing and pipe and often catch it from their dear father. Some business!

Once again, Marx showed his aptitude for the law. He exposed most of the handwritten evidence against

A scene from the trial of the Cologne Communists, 1852. Despite Marx's best efforts, the men were convicted and sentenced to prison terms, helping convince Marx to formally dissolve the Communist League.

the defendants as forgeries, and he argued that under the French civil code still in force in Cologne, the mere possession of writings such as *The Communist Manifesto* was not a criminal offense. Marx's campaign to free the accused Communists ultimately proved fruitless, however. In late 1852, after a five-week trial, most of the defendants were found guilty and sentenced to prison terms of between three and six years. Five days later, at Marx's request, the Communist League was formally dissolved.

In the midst of the commotion in Cologne, Marx had again been deceived by a spy. In 1852, Marx and Engels wrote "The Great Men of Exile," a polemical account of the petty feuds between exiled members of the German democracy movement in London. Marx gave the manuscript to the Hungarian Janos Bangya, who assured him that he had found a publisher for the text in Germany. It turned out that Bangya was actually an Austrian spy. He probably sold the manuscript to the Prussian police.

Marx took care to avoid becoming embroiled in the revolutionary plots continually being hatched by members of the German exile community. But he never gave up his hope of seeing a revolution, which he thought would break out in the wake of a major financial and economic crisis. Until the revolution came, Marx planned to work on his "scientific" studies of capitalism.

Marx's personal experience of the capitalist system—and the great inequalities and misery it engendered—was acute. London during the time was a teeming metropolitan district of about 2.5 million people. Trade and finance had created huge wealth for some, and the

upper classes lived in sumptu-
ous mansions and strolled
through large, well-manicured
parks. Yet hundreds of thou-
sands of workers and the
unemployed lived in crowded,
filthy slums.

In general, life for German
emigrants was difficult. Some
who had worked in a trade in
Germany—tailors, cobblers,
carpenters, watchmakers, type-
setters, and the like—managed
to find employment. Marx,
however, had no marketable
skills, and only once did he
even try to land a job—a cleri-

Jenny Marx, like her husband, always tried to maintain an air of middle-class respectability. This photograph is from about 1850.

cal position at a railway station. He was rejected because
no one could read his handwriting.

After the Marxes' first months in London, aid from
refugee committees ceased. Marx had to borrow from
friends, sign bills, and chalk up debts with bakers,
butchers, apothecaries, and even the milkman, all in
the expectation that he would settle his affairs soon. In
May 1850 the wretchedness of existence, as Marx
called his domestic misery, was revealed in a letter
Jenny wrote to Engels. There was a sick baby Jenny
couldn't adequately nurse, quarrels with the landlady
over unpaid rent that led to the family's eviction, small
lenders who besieged the family with unpaid bills. They
found shelter in the house of a Jewish lace dealer, where

they spent a miserable summer while Jenny was pregnant again and constantly ill.

Marx was hoping for help from his wealthy maternal uncle Lion Philips, who ran a business in a small Dutch town. In August 1850, Marx sent his pregnant wife—his uncle was not exactly a fan of revolutions—to beg his uncle for money. Philips treated Jenny with kindness, but she was unable to extract any money from him. When in desperation she pointed out that the family might have to emigrate to America, Philips declared that an excellent idea.

Marx started to think about publishing a magazine in New York. It did not take him long to scrap the plan because he discovered that tickets for the voyage were too expensive. He seems to have been unaware that the British Home Office was prepared to give financial assistance to refugees wishing to emigrate to the United States.

Friedrich Engels turned out to be the financial guardian angel of the Marx family. Engels scaled back his journalistic and political ambitions and joined the Manchester office of his father's textile firm, Ermen & Engels. He remained there for almost twenty years. Engels had not wanted to become a businessman, but he played his role very well, eventually being promoted to partner and gaining a significant income. Before that promotion, however, his salary was modest. To support his friend Marx in those years, Engels frequently stole from the company's petty cash box or withdrew money in small denominations from the company's bank account. Neither his father nor his business partner in

Manchester, Peter Ermen, ever found out about the thievery.

Engels sent notes of five pounds to Marx, which he cut in half and posted in two different letters in order to avoid mail theft. In addition to the money, Engels provided confidential details of the cotton trade and expert observations on the state of international markets, which were invaluable to Marx in his studies of capitalism.

From 1852, Marx was able to make some money of his own by writing for the *New-York Daily Tribune*. At almost 200,000 copies a day, the newspaper was the largest-circulation daily paper in the world. Marx was hired to write a series of articles about the strategy and tactics of the Prussian and Austrian armies during the revolutions of 1848. However, there was a problem. Marx couldn't write well in English and had little or no clue about military affairs, but the offer of one pound per article tempted him. Again Engels—whom the Marx family nicknamed "the General" because he knew so much about military matters—came to the rescue. He wrote the first articles for Marx.

Marx improved his English and went on to write his own articles for the *Tribune* as its Europe correspondent. About 500 articles dealing with the character of revolutionary crisis were published under his name, although Engels wrote many of them. Marx's major source for facts was the *London Times*.

When not writing his articles for the *Tribune*, Marx spent innumerable hours engaged in his scientific study of capitalism. He did most of his research at the library of the British Museum, which had granted him a library card in 1850. His work may have approached the level of obsession, but Marx was by all accounts a devoted family man who adored his wife and was very fond of his children.

A Prussian spy who had apparently won Marx's trust wrote a vivid description of Marx and the family's house on Dean Street in the early 1850s:

As father and husband, Marx, in spite of his wild and restless character, is the gentlest and mildest of men. Marx lives in one of the worst, therefore one of the cheapest quarters of London. He occupies two rooms. The one looking out on the street is the salon, and the bedroom is at the back. In the whole apartment, there is not one clean and solid piece of furniture. Everything is broken, tattered and torn, with a half inch of dust over everything and the greatest disorder everywhere. In the middle of the salon there is a large old-fashioned table covered with an oilcloth, and on it there lie manuscripts, books and newspapers, as well as the children's toys, the rags and tatters of his wife's sewing basket, several cups with broken rims, knives, forks, lamps, an inkpot, tumblers, Dutch clay pipes, tobacco ash—in a word, everything topsy-turvy, and all on the same table. A seller of second-hand goods would be ashamed to give away such a remarkable collection of odds and ends.

When you enter Marx's room smoke and tobacco fumes make your eyes water so much that for a moment you seem to be groping about in a cavern, but gradually, as you grow accustomed to the fog, you can make out certain objects which distinguish themselves from the surrounding haze. Everything is dirty, and covered with dust, so that to sit down becomes a thoroughly dangerous business. Here is a chair with only three legs, on another chair the children are playing at cooking—this chair happens to have four legs. This is the one which is offered to the visitor, but the children's cooking has not been wiped away; and if you sit down, you risk a pair of trousers.

The disorder inside their house notwithstanding, the Marx family almost desperately tried to maintain the illusion of a middle-class existence. They could have lived rather decently with the money Engels and other friends sent them, but both Karl and Jenny Marx repeatedly spent beyond their means. Jenny wasn't willing to give up completely the life she had led as an aristocratic girl. She had personal cards printed with her married name and "née Baronesse Westphalen" (born Baroness Westphalen). When money was available, Jenny bought new dresses for her daughters and the family went on holidays. At times Marx even hired a male secretary, Wilhelm Pieper, who had little command of written English and therefore could only copy but certainly not decently translate Marx's articles.

When the last penny was gone—something that happened all too often—the family sent virtually everything they owned to the pawnshop. Sometimes Marx had not a single suit left at home and could not leave the house. Once he even spent a weekend in jail because a pawnshop owner questioned the origin of Jenny's silver and alerted the police. Marx's children were used to telling creditors at the door: "Mr. Marx is not here."

Often the Marx family had to survive on potatoes, the only food they could afford. Malnourishment and poverty took a heavy toll. Illnesses in the family were frequent. Two of the Marx children—son Guido (born in 1849) and daughter Franziska (born in 1851)—died at age one. The family couldn't even afford a coffin for Franziska, but a compassionate French refugee paid for one. In 1856 the Marxes' son Edgar died of tuberculosis at age six. Marx had been especially fond of Edgar, a very intelligent boy,

A drawing of Edgar Marx, who died of tuberculosis at the age of six. Marx was devastated by the loss of his beloved son.

and was devastated by the loss. At the funeral Marx's friend Wilhelm Liebknecht closely watched over the heartbroken father, fearing that he might jump into the open grave when the little coffin of his son was lowered. One year after Edgar's death, another child of Karl and Jenny Marx died at birth. Of the couple's seven children, only three daughters—Jenny Caroline, Laura, and Eleanor—remained.

Karl Marx had fathered another child, however. In 1850, while his wife was in the midst of a deep depression, Marx had found comfort in the arms of Lenchen Demuth, the family's faithful housekeeper. By the spring of 1851, it was obvious Demuth was pregnant, but she steadfastly refused to name the father. On June 23 she gave birth to a boy, Frederick, who was given to foster parents. Amid a swirl of rumors, Engels eventually claimed to be the boy's father in order to spare Marx from the scandal.

In 1857, almost a decade after the revolutions of 1848 had swept through Europe, a financial panic sent the European economies into free fall. Marx believed that the revolution he had long anticipated was at hand. From October 1857 to March 1858, he frantically wrote a manuscript that filled seven notebooks and reached eight hundred pages. The surviving manuscript became known as the *"Grundrisse,"* from the first word of the German title "Grundrisse der Kritik der politischen Oekonomie" (Outlines of a critique of political economy). The *Grundrisse* wasn't published until the mid-twentieth century, at which time scholars could see how the outlines helped lay the foundation for Marx's most important work, *Das Kapital*, or *Capital*. The wide-ranging outlines are impossible to describe succinctly. Some of the most interesting passages include Marx's view that the wealth of capitalism was based on the introduction of machinery followed by that of automation.

Once again, Marx was short on cash. He joked to Engels that he did not suppose anyone had ever written so much about money who had so little. Jenny had received a small inheritance from her mother, enabling the family to move from the cramped house on Dean Street to a larger home on Grafton Terrace in Kentish Town, which was then a northern suburb of London, in 1856. But the new place was well beyond the Marx family's means.

Marx pushed himself relentlessly, reading and writing well into most nights while smoking one cigar after another. His health began to suffer.

In 1860 Jenny contracted smallpox, and Marx hired a nurse to look after his wife. "I lay constantly by the open window," Jenny later wrote of her illness, "so that the cold November air would blow over me, while there was a raging fire in the stove and burning ice on my lips, and I was given drops of claret from time to time. I could hardly swallow, my hearing was getting weaker, and finally my eyes closed, so that I did not know

Karl Marx, 1861.

whether I would remain enveloped in eternal night." Jenny survived, but she was left partially deaf, and her skin was marked with scars. Her emotional reserves, too, seemed spent; she now found it especially difficult to cope during the frequent periods of financial trouble.

The years 1862 and 1863 were especially desperate for Marx. The American Civil War had cut off the supply of cotton, sending Britain's textile industry into depression. Engels was no longer able to give money to his friend. In a plaintive letter to Engels, Marx seemed to express regret that he had devoted his life to study rather than pursuing a paying career. "Grey, dear friend, is all theory and only business is green," Marx wrote. "Unfortunately, I have come too late to this insight."

Marx almost managed to drive away his best friend. In January 1863, Engels wrote a letter informing Marx that his longtime companion, Mary Burns, had died. Marx replied with a letter that was both crass and devoid of sympathy. Why, he asked Engels, had Mary Burns died and not Marx's own mother, who was sitting on his inheritance? Engels's reply showed how deeply Marx's mundane thoughts about money had hurt him, and Marx wrote a sincere apology letter—probably the only one in his life. Days later Engels scraped together some money and saved the Marx family from bankruptcy once again.

When news came in November 1863 that Marx's mother had finally passed away at the age of seventy-five, Marx reacted coolly. Engels had to pay for his trip to Trier. Once all advances and loans had been paid, Marx's share of her estate totaled little more than 100 pounds. Still, Marx decided to take a three-year lease on a spacious mansion with an annual rent of 65 pounds, almost twice that of his current house.

However, good fortune came again when Wilhelm Wolff, an old ally of Marx and Engels, died in May 1864 and left them all of his possessions. Marx reaped a windfall of 820 pounds, which was far more than he had ever earned from his writing.

It is one of the ironies of Marx's life that he survived on the bourgeois institution of inheritances, which in his *Communist Manifesto* he had said should be abolished. It seems that capitalism's most relentless critic wasn't above playing the markets either. In the summer of 1864, Marx sent a letter to Lion Philips in which he proudly informed his wealthy uncle that he had been speculating in stocks.

For a while, the Marx family was able to enjoy a rather bourgeois lifestyle in their new home, which they furnished and redecorated. Marx even held a grand ball there for his daughters Jenny Caroline and Laura. But by July 1865 he was once again broke. Most of the household items had to be pawned before Engels again came to the rescue.

Marx had signed a letter of understanding with the Hamburg publisher Otto Meissner to produce four books in three volumes. When the 1865 deadline passed and Marx had not yet submitted any finished work, the publisher started to write unfriendly letters. Battling health problems and struggling to keep his creditors at bay, Marx managed to produce a large manuscript. The book, thoroughly revised and amended by Engels, was finally published in September 1867. Its German title was *Das Kapital*.

It is impossible to sum up the contents of Marx's major work in a few sentences. Broadly, *Capital* is a critical analysis of capitalism, whose driving force, according to Marx, rested in the alienation and exploitation of labor. Capitalist profits, in Marx's analysis, ultimately derived from the uncompensated labor of wage workers. His argument, in highly simplified form, was as follows. The value of a product rests in how much labor is needed to make that product. An item that requires more labor to produce, Marx said, is worth more than an item that requires less labor to produce. Furthermore, if the daily labor of a worker generates products that are sold for, say, $50, then the worker should receive a daily wage of $50 (minus the cost of the materials). But that is not the case. The product always sells at a price higher than the cost of the materials and the wages paid to the worker. In Marx's view, this was how capitalists made profits and continually accumulated more capi-

Jenny Caroline (left) and Laura Marx, 1864. That year, a windfall inheritance from his friend Wilhelm Wolff enabled Marx to move his family into a mansion and give his daughters a grand ball.

tal—they unfairly took the "surplus value" created by wage workers.

Modern economists have shown that much of Marx's thinking was wrong. His notion that the value of a product is determined by the amount of labor necessary to produce it, for example, doesn't jibe with observed reality. A prospector might work for ten minutes before finding a large nugget of gold, and a factory worker might spend fifteen minutes making a pair of sneakers, but the gold is worth a lot more than the sneakers. Where there are free markets, a product is worth what someone is willing to pay for it. Marx's belief that it was exploitative not to pay workers the full value

The cover of *Das Kapital*. Marx's most important—and most impenetrable—book was first published in 1867.

of the finished products (minus material costs) is similarly problematic. Capital is required for, among other things, setting up and maintaining factories, managing the workforce, and marketing and distributing products. None of these things could be done if capitalists paid workers the full value of the products they produced. In addition, without the prospect of earning profits, there would be no incentive for capitalists to go into business in the first place. So workers wouldn't have jobs.

Despite its flaws, *Capital* is an important work with many valuable insights. Still, outside of scholarly circles, it is not widely read today. That is largely because of its barely coherent organization, nineteenth-century terminology, and tedious level of detail. The book is often referred to as an unfinished masterpiece plagued by formlessness and incomprehensibility. The most dramatic and readable parts paint a ghastly picture of early capitalism in Victorian England. The account sometimes resembles a Gothic novel with dripping blood and capitalism as a monster consuming work slaves. The book ends with an apocalyptic vision. Capitalism, Marx said, would inevitably destroy itself, and days of the capitalists were already numbered.

The German public reacted coolly to Marx's rambling mix of economic theory, social history, sociology, and propaganda. When not ignored entirely, *Capital* was almost always misunderstood. A telling example is that of a Russian censor who allowed the book to pass because it did not call for revolution—and workers would not understand it anyway.

It took four years to sell the thousand copies of the first edition in Germany. Engels managed to place reviews in a variety of German newspapers, but they bore little fruit. Marx, plagued by ill health, panicked at the thought of having to produce the next two volumes. But that would not happen because, once again, Marx had allowed himself to be dragged into another political fight.

9 The Political Fighter

After the dissolution of the Communist League in 1852, Marx had avoided political commitments. However, by the early 1860s political and economic conditions encouraged a revival of working-class activity in Europe. In England, organized trade unions had sprung up. In France, Napoleon III relaxed anti-trade-union laws. Even in Germany, there was a new working-class movement.

In 1861 the new Prussian king had announced an amnesty for Prussian citizens involved in the revolutions of 1848. Marx could finally travel to Berlin. His idea was to found a weekly paper there with Ferdinand Lassalle, who had sent a cash advance. Marx had known Lassalle since his days in Cologne. Lassalle, son of a Jewish tailor from Breslau in Silesia, was seven years younger than Marx and had long admired him.

A wealthy man, Lassalle wined and dined Marx, taking him to parties and to the opera. Berlin society did not impress Marx, however. Most of the time, he was terribly bored. His major wish—getting his Prussian citizenship back—was denied, and the future of the weekly paper was left undecided after Lassalle offered to finance the paper only under the condition that he edit it jointly with Marx. Marx did not like rivals. He left the country with the sarcastic comment that Germany was such a beautiful land that he preferred to live outside its borders.

Lassalle's visit to London's World Exposition of 1862 turned out to be a total disaster. Once again, Marx was in financial trouble and could not afford to entertain his demanding guest. While Marx fought to fend off his creditors, Lassalle behaved like a boastful big spender. However, he

Ferdinand Lassalle, a prominent socialist, planned to co-edit a newspaper with Marx. But the two men were unable to get along with each other.

was unwilling to help Marx out financially. It became obvious that collaboration between the two incompatible persons was out of the question. Marx wrote disdainful and even anti-Semitic comments about Lassalle to Engels.

In May 1863, Lassalle founded the General Union of German Workers (ADAV). Its major demands were universal suffrage in Prussia and the formation of state-subsidized factories, which would distribute the accumulated profits to the workers. The ADAV would later merge with the Social Democratic Workers' Party of Germany. Lassalle wrote a declaration of worker demands that bore a considerable resemblance to *The Communist Manifesto*, and Marx complained that Lassalle had copied some of his ideas. The rivalry between the two men ended in 1864, when Lassalle was killed in a duel with a Romanian aristocrat.

Labor unrest continued to foment. In September 1864, the International Workingmen's Association (IWA) was founded in London at St. Martin's Hall. One of its goals was to prevent the importation of foreign workers in order to break strikes. The International, as the IWA was often called, proved to be quite successful in that respect. Within a week, Marx wrote an "Address to the Working Classes," which took up a few

Marx and his daughters with Friedrich Engels (back, left) in London. In 1869, after selling his share in the textile company, Engels granted Marx an annual pension of 350 pounds. The following year, Engels moved into a mansion close to Marx's home.

points from *The Communist Manifesto* but refrained from sweeping generalizations or appeals to revolutionary action.

Marx felt that the emancipation of the working classes had to be achieved by the working classes themselves. Their struggle, he believed, would eventually lead to the abolition of all class distinctions. A central point of his address was that no improvement of machinery, no application of science to production, no contrivance of communication, no new colonies, no emigration, no opening of markets, and no free trade would do away with the miseries of industrial workers. Every fresh development of the productive powers of labor would only sharpen social contrasts and accentuate social antagonisms. Marx closed with his traditional appeal: "Proletarians of all countries, unite!"

The "Address to the Working Classes" contained many elements Marx later worked out in *Capital*. The members of the IWA liked the text so much that Marx was charged with writing many more documents and resolutions. Without being its official leader Marx, who was elected to every succeeding General Council of the association, became the undisputed mentor of the IWA.

Marx showed remarkable diplomatic skills in holding together the IWA, an alliance of people from diverse groups. While Marx believed that the German working class would be the vanguard of a proletarian revolution, the International had its largest base in France.

The Brussels Congress of the International called for a general strike should there be a war, which Marx thought of as an empty declaration because the working class still was not organized enough to hold a mass strike. When the Franco-Prussian War broke out in July 1870, the IWA only issued a prudent declaration, written by Marx, that warned against an escalation of the conflict. A second declaration of the General Council called upon the workers of both countries to engage in an active struggle for peace because passivity of the workers would lead to even more catastrophic wars in the future.

In September 1870, Engels wrote Marx that if the workers attempted a revolutionary rising they would be crushed, and the workers' movement would be set back another twenty years. Marx took note and warned the French workers not to topple the French provisional government that had been formed after the defeat of Napoleon III at Sedan, because the workers would only weaken themselves. His advice was not heeded. On March 18, 1871, an uprising of discontented French workers broke out. It led to the Paris Commune, the short-lived reformist government of the city. The Commune introduced reform measures and tried to pave the way for a progressive social democracy, but it shied away from full-scale social revolution.

Despite his efforts to keep his distance from the Paris Commune, Marx was seen by some as being behind it. The London press, for example, claimed that the General Council of the International, headed by Marx, had instigated and organized the uprising in Paris.

By May 1871, the Paris Commune would be crushed. Marx's address to the Commune, a pamphlet of some forty pages subtitled "The Civil War in France," was in fact an obituary. The document reveals more about Marx's view of a future Communist society than about the current Paris Commune. "Working men's Paris, with its Commune, will be forever celebrated as the glorious harbinger of a new society," Marx wrote. "The martyrs are enshrined in the great heart of the working class. Its exterminator's history has already nailed to that eternal pillory from which all the prayers of their priests will not avail to redeem them."

The pamphlet, published anonymously, was quickly translated into many languages. Later it provided Lenin

A heroic and somewhat overwrought painting of the last stand of the Paris Commune. The short-lived Commune, Marx wrote, would "be forever celebrated as the glorious harbinger of a new society."

in Russia with a basis for the Bolshevik view of the dictatorship of the proletariat.

The anonymous author of "The Civil War in France" was soon found out. Suddenly Marx, who had been virtually unknown in England, became notorious. He was interviewed by major British and American newspapers. His pamphlet, he said, was "making the devil of a noise and I have the honor to be at this moment the most abused and threatened man in London. That really does me good after the tedious twenty-year idyll in my den!"

The newly formed German Reich's ambassador in London demanded that Marx be tried as a common criminal. Voices were raised in the British House of Commons to move against the IWA. After looking into the matter, the British Home Secretary decided that Marx and his followers were harmless malcontents.

The best days of the IWA were behind it, however. Europeans became more focused on the affairs of their own countries, the idea of internationalism held less appeal, and revolutionary enthusiasm declined. The

Marx and his daughter Jenny Caroline. Her death, coming barely a year after the death of his wife, was a crushing blow for Marx. Within two months, he too would die.

General Council of the IWA was soon plagued by internal bickering. In Geneva, the Russian anarchist Mikhail Bakunin had split the local section and formed his own organization.

The Fifth Congress of the International, held in September 1872, was the only one Marx personally attended. The meeting showed how much members were at odds with one another. While Marx had managed to have Bakunin expelled, he was fed up. Marx had Engels propose that the seat of the General Council be transferred to New York to protect it from disintegrating elements. Marx fully realized that he was sounding the death knell of the IWA. Four years later, the group was formally dissolved in Philadelphia.

Marx now had two fewer things to worry about. His "slavery" to the IWA was over, and from 1869 until his death he enjoyed a pension of 350 pounds granted by Engels, who had sold his part in the textile company. In 1870 Engels moved into a mansion close to Marx's home. The two friends could see each other almost daily. Marx thought he'd go back to his writing. However, his creative days were over.

Marx's final years, though spent in improved material circumstances, were shadowed by grief. In December 1881, his beloved wife, Jenny, died of cancer. In January 1883, Marx endured the death of his oldest daughter, Jenny Caroline, who fell victim to cancer at the age of thirty-eight.

Two months after his daughter's death, on March 14, 1883, Karl Marx died in his armchair at his house in London. He was sixty-five.

10 Legacy

arx was buried in London's Highgate Cemetery on March 17, 1883. Only eleven mourners were in attendance. Friedrich Engels delivered a funeral oration in which he summed up the life's work of his friend. "Marx was before all else a revolutionist," Engels declared. "His real mission in life was to contribute, in one way or another, to the overthrow of capitalist society and of the state institutions which it had brought into being, to contribute to the liberation of the modern proletariat, which he was the first to make conscious of its own position and its needs, conscious of the conditions of its emancipation."

Marx the revolutionist died without seeing the overthrow of a single capitalist society. Four decades later, following the Russian Revolution, the Bolsheviks came to power in Russia and, under the leadership of Lenin, established the Union of Soviet Socialist Republics. The Soviet Union's governing ideology was a mix of Marx's ideas and those of Lenin, and it is therefore usually referred to as Marxism-Leninism.

Marx had predicted that the overthrow of capitalism would be followed by a "dictatorship of the proletariat"—

a temporary stage that would give way to the establishment of pure communism. Under communism, society would be completely classless, social relations would be harmonious, and every person would share equally in the material prosperity.

This vision was never realized—in the Soviet Union or in any of the other countries that had Communist governments. State control of the means of production, a key element of Marx's economic philosophy, turned out to be highly inefficient. The Communist countries all suffered chronic shortages of goods, industrial innovation was stifled, and standards of living lagged behind those in capitalist countries.

Communism's champion in old age. "The philosophers," Marx once famously said, "have only interpreted the world in various ways; the point is to change it."

Nor were any of the Communist countries classless. Invariably, a privileged ruling class made up of members of the Communist Party arose.

But most significantly, Communist societies were anything but harmonious. Almost without exception, Communist governments were highly repressive. Political rights were nonexistent, and citizens who criticized the ruling regime risked imprisonment or death.

Vladimir Lenin (1870–1924) dedicates a monument to Marx and Engels, November 1918. Lenin adapted Marx's ideas about Communism, using them as the basis for a new government after leading the Bolshevik takeover of Russia in late 1917. His innovations, known as Marxism-Leninism, became the dominant ideology in the Union of Soviet Socialist Republics (USSR).

During the 1930s, Soviet leader Joseph Stalin had millions of people executed or deliberately starved to death in order to consolidate his power. Millions died in China during Mao Zedong's Cultural Revolution (1966–76). The Communist Khmer Rouge systematically murdered an estimated 1.5 million men, women, and children in Cambodia between 1975 and 1979.

Karl Marx was a lifelong opponent of oppression and a champion of freedom and social justice. It is safe to say that he would have been horrified to see all that had been done in his name.

By the late 1980s, communism was collapsing. In November 1989, the Berlin Wall fell, and in quick succession the Soviet-dominated countries of Eastern

Europe got rid of their Communist governments. The Soviet Union itself dissolved in December 1991. While the Chinese Communist Party remains in control politically, China has adopted a capitalist economic system— and its economy has boomed. Today, Marxist ideology is followed in a reasonably faithful way only in the small and isolated countries of Cuba and North Korea.

Given these developments, it might be tempting to dismiss Marx and his work as irrelevant. After all, he predicted the downfall of capitalism and the inevitable triumph of communism. That has not happened, and there appears to be little chance that it ever will.

But Marx was right about several things. He foresaw the concentration of wealth under capitalism. Today, the richest 1 percent of people in the world own more than 40 percent of all global assets, while more than one-fifth of the world's people live in extreme poverty. Marx also accurately predicted the "universal interdependence of nations"—or what is today known as globalization.

Marx's most fundamental contribution, though, was in recognizing the importance of material circumstances in the development of human society. As Engels put it in his funeral oration, "Marx discovered the law of development of human history: the simple fact, hitherto concealed by an overgrowth of ideology, that mankind must first of all eat, drink, have shelter and clothing, before it can pursue politics, science, art, religion."

Time Line

1818: Karl Heinrich Marx is born May 5 in Trier, Germany.

1830: Attends Friedrich-Wilhelm-Gymnasium in Trier.

1835: Begins law studies at University of Bonn.

1836: Moves to University of Berlin.

1841: Receives doctorate from University of Jena.

1842: Becomes editor of the Rheinische Zeitung in Cologne.

1843: Marries Jenny von Westphalen.

1844: Edits the *German-French Yearbooks* in Paris.

1845: Moves to Brussels and loses Prussian citizenship.

1846: Finishes *The German Ideology*.

1847: Attacks the French socialist Pierre-Joseph Proudhon in *The Poverty of Philosophy*.

1848: Publishes *The Communist Manifesto*.

1849: Moves to exile in London.

1852: Publishes *The Eighteenth Brumaire of Louis Napoleon*.

1857: Writes the first draft of *Capital*.

1861: Meets Ferdinand Lassalle in Berlin.

1864: Becomes the acknowledged head of the International.

1867: Publishes the first volume of *Capital*.

1871: Publishes "The Civil War in France."

1883: Dies March 14 in London.

Source Notes

For abbreviations see Bibliography, Collected Editions, page 106

1: Early Years

p. 10,   "we cannot always attain . . ." MECW I, 4.

p. 11,   "According to History the greatest . . ." Ibid.

2: The Student

p. 17,   "Although I am very pleased . . ." MEW, Suppl. I, 621.

p. 19,   "When I left you . . ." David McLellan, ed., *Karl Marx,
Early Texts* (Oxford: Blackwell, 1971), 2.

p. 22,   "grotesque and rocky melody," Ibid., 7.

4: The Journalist

p. 33,   "If every violation of property . . ." McLellan, *Early Texts*,
49.

5: Revolution Approaches

p. 38,   "The true relationship of thought . . ." David McLellan,
Karl Marx: A Biography (London: Palgrave McMillan,
2006), 64.

p. 43,   "plunged again and again . . ." Franz Mehring, *Karl Marx,
the Story of His Life* (London: Allen and Unwin, 1951), 74.

p. 47,   "I fear that in the end . . ." Francis Wheen, *Karl Marx*
(London: Fourth Estate, 2000), 91.

6: The Revolutionary

p. 50,   "In communist society . . ." Karl Marx and Friedrich
Engels, *The German Ideology* (Moscow: Institute of
Marxism-Leninism, 1965), 45.

p. 50, "These times will come . . ." Wheen, *Karl Marx*, 97.

p. 52, "behaved disloyally . . ." Werner Blumenberg, *Karl Marx: An Illustrated History*, translated by Douglas Scott (London: Verso, 1998), 59.

p. 53, "Marx himself was the type . . ." McLellan, *Karl Marx*, 426.

p. 54, "equivalent to vain dishonest . . ." *Reminiscences of Marx and Engels* (Moscow: Foreign Languages Publishing House, 1960), 170.

p. 55, "M. Proudhon the economist . . ." Wheen, *Karl Marx*, 108.

p. 57, "Marx was then still . . ." *Reminiscences of Marx and Engels,* 153.

7: The Communist Manifesto

p. 58, "If the Manifesto . . ." Wheen, *Karl Marx*, 119.

p. 60, "A spectre is haunting Europe . . ." Karl Marx and Friedrich Engels, *The Communist Manifesto*, introduction by A. J. P. Taylor (New York: Penguin, 1981), 78.

p. 60, "The history of all hitherto . . ." Ibid., 79.

p. 60, "In the earlier epochs . . ." Ibid., 80.

p. 62, "have no interests separate . . ." Ibid., 95.

p. 62   "the theory of the Communists . . ." Ibid., 96.

p. 63, "The Communists disdain to conceal . . ." Ibid., 120–21.

p. 64, "The soil of the French Republic . . ." MEW XXIV, 676.

8: The Economist

p. 75, "My husband had to work . . ." MEW XXVII, 461.

p. 80, "As father and husband . . ." McLellan, *Karl Marx*, 246.

p. 83, "I lay constantly . . ." *Reminiscences of Marx and Engels,* 247.

p. 84, "Grey, dear friend, is all theory . . ." MEW XXX, 280.

9: The Politician

p. 93, "Proletarians of all countries, unite!" Karl Marx, "Inaugural Address of the International Working Men's Association." http://www.marxists.org/archive/marx/works/1864/10/27.htm

p. 95, "Working men's Paris . . ." MESW I, 541.

p. xx, "making the devil of a noise . . ." MEW XXXIII, 238.

10: Legacy

p. 98, "Marx was before all . . ." Friedrich Engels, "Karl Marx's Funeral" (*Der Sozialdemokrat*, March 22, 1883). http://www.marxists.org/archive/marx/works/1883/death/de rsoz1.htm.

p. 98 "dictatorship of the proletariat" Karl Marx, *The Portable Karl Marx*, ed. Eugene Kamenka (New York: Viking Penguin, 1983), 550.

p. 99, "The philosophers have only interpreted . . ." Marx and Engels, *The German Ideology*, 28.

p. 101 "universal interdependence of nations" Marx, *The Portable Karl Marx*, 208.

p. 101, "Marx discovered the law . . ." Engels, "Karl Marx's Funeral."

Bibliography

Collected Editions, in German

Karl Marx and Friedrich Engels. *Werke*, edited by the Institute for Marxism-Leninism. Berlin/East: Dietz Verlag, 1956-68 (MEW).

——. *Gesamtausgabe*. Berlin: Akademie Verlag, 1975. (MEGA)

Collected Editions, in English

Karl Marx and Friedrich Engels. *Selected Works*. Moscow: Co-operative Publishing Society of Foreign Workers in the U.S.S.R, 1935. (MESW)

——. *Collected Works*. Moscow, New York, and London: International Publishers, 1975-2005. (MECW)

——. *The German Ideology*, Moscow: Institute of Marxism-Leninism, 1965.

Karl Marx, *Early Texts*, ed. D. McLellan. Oxford: Blackwell, 1971.

Reminiscences of Marx and Engels, Moscow: Foreign Languages Publishing House, 1960.

Biographical Works

Attali, Jacques. *Karl Marx ou l'esprit du monde*. Paris: Fayard, 2005.

Berlin, Isaiah. *Marx. His Life and Environment*, Oxford: Oxford University Press, 1968.

Blumenberg, Werner. *Karl Marx. An Illustrated History*. London, New York: Verso, 2000.

Körner, Klaus. *Karl Marx*. Munich: Deutscher Taschenbuch Verlag, 2008.

McLellan, David. *Karl Marx. A Biography*. London: Palgrave McMillan, 1972, Fourth Edition 2006.

Mehring, Franz. *Karl Marx, the Story of His Life*. London: Allen and Unwin, 1951.

Wheen, Francis. *Karl Marx*. London: Fourth Estate, 2000.

——. *Marx's Das Kapital*. London: Atlantic Books, 2006.

Websites

http://www.marxists.org/archive/marx/works/cw/

Listing of the Marx/Engels Collected Works (MECW), as compiled and printed by Progress Publishers of the Soviet Union in collaboration with Lawrence & Wishart (London) and International Publishers (New York), starting in 1975 and completed in 2005. This compilation is the most complete publication of the works of Marx/Engels in English.

http://www.fes.de/marx/index_e.htm

Exhibition in the Museum-Karl-Marx-Haus run by the German Social Democratic Party which provides information about Karl Marx's life, work, and influence from the end of the nineteenth century to the present day.

http://www.iisg.nl/imes/

The International Institute of Social History established the Internationale Marx-Engels-Stiftung (IMES) in 1990. This network brings together the most important centers of Marx and Engels studies and continues the publication of the Marx-Engels-Gesamtausgabe

Index

Numbers in **bold italics** refer to captions.

Picture Credits